Niels Lehmann & Christoph Rauhut

FRAGMENTS OF METROPOLIS EAST | OST

The Expressionist Heritage in Poland, the Czech Republic and Slovakia

Das expressionistische Erbe in Polen, Tschechien und der Slowakei

HIRMER

Heterogeneous and without apparent precedent — what we show in this third volume of "Fragments of Metropolis" does not seem, at first, to be part of a common architectural movement, but rather the collage of several. Such an impression is not entirely mistaken, because the architecture of the interwar period in central Eastern Europe was markedly bound to its various regional political, economic and cultural contexts. Political upheaval and a heightened awareness of national identity, combined with regional building traditions, led to different currents of a 'new' art of building in the region, which, though flourishing at different times, all culminated in an expressive architectural language. In its initially heterogeneous overall view, this book thus also presents what they have common: an art of building that offers an answer to the contemporary epochal break, through explicitly modern, sculptural design, while at the same time not completely abandoning the historically transmitted vocabulary of architecture. Together with the other volumes in this series, the fragments presented here document how significant and formative this approach was to architecture in the early twentieth century.

Niels Lehmann & Christoph Rauhut

Heterogen und ohne direkte Bezüge – was wir im dritten Band der Reihe »Fragments of Metropolis« zeigen, scheint auf den ersten Blick nicht Teil einer gemeinsamen Architekturbewegung zu sein, sondern eher die Collage mehrerer. Ein solcher Eindruck ist auch nicht falsch, denn die Architektur der Zwischenkriegszeit im mittelöstlichen Europa kennzeichnet eine starke Bindung an regionale politische, wirtschaftliche wie auch kulturelle Kontexte. Politische Umbrüche und ein gesteigertes Bewusstsein von nationalen Identitäten, verbunden mit regionalen Bautraditionen, führten zu unterschiedlichen Strömungen einer »neuen« (Bau-)Kunst in dieser Großregion, die – zeitlich versetzt – alle in einer expressiven Architektursprache mündeten. In seiner zunächst heterogenen Gesamtschau präsentiert das Buch damit auch das Gemeinsame: Eine Baukunst, die über eine explizit moderne, plastische Gestaltung versucht, eine Antwort auf den zeitgenössischen Epochenbruch zu geben, und gleichzeitig das historisch überlieferte Vokabular der Architektur nicht gänzlich aufgibt. Gemeinsam mit den anderen Bänden dokumentieren die hier vorgestellten Fragmente, wie bedeutsam und prägend dieser Ansatz für die Architektur des beginnenden 20. Jahrhunderts war.

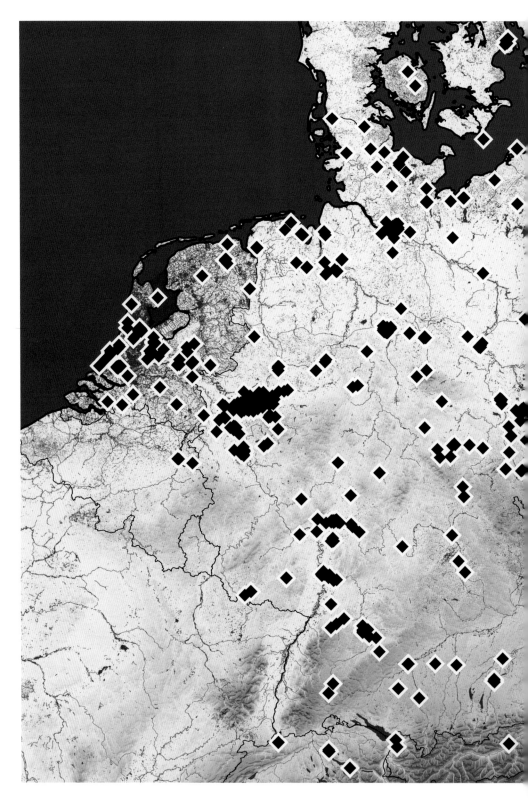

North | Norden, Netherlands | Niederlande, Berlin (published |
erschienen), Rhein & Ruhr (published | erschienen), East | Osten,
Central Germany | Mitteldeutschland, South | Süden

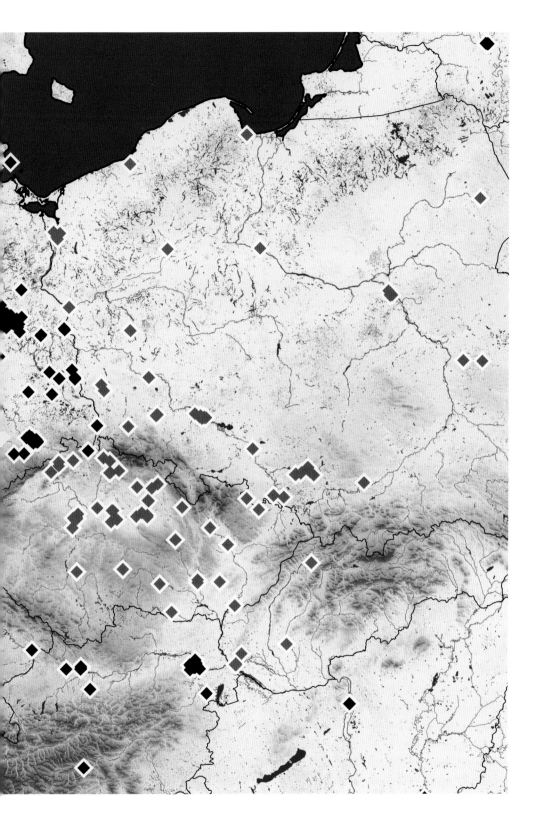

CONTENTS
INHALT

Gesine Schwan

HOMELAND METROPOLIS

In a time when a cry for 'homeland' rings
out against the diversity and multiculturalism that
globalisation brings, a book such as this is a wel-
come appearance. Firstly, simply because it brings
together such wonderful photographs of Expressionist monuments, which even aesthetically are
a joy to behold. Distinguished villas, churches,
synagogues, urban housing, cinemas, theatres,
swimming baths — even power stations — all exude
the colourful vitality and elegance of Expressionist
architecture.

But this publication also demonstrates
that homeland does not always necessarily lie in
opposition to the diversity and openness of a world
city: Unlike those reactionary, often regressive desires to withdraw into unaltered and unchangeable
surroundings — somewhere you've always known,
within which an idea of homeland is held onto —
this architectural style invites us to take part in the
experimentation and curiosity of the bustling life
to be found in the metropolis (even though Expressionist architecture spread far beyond the great
metropolises), where the most diverse collection
of people meet, each with their own experiences,
ideas and desires. Metropolis is the attractive alternative to a closed society, whose 'security' comes at
the expense of the boredom of the continual return
to the known and the conventional.

This bustling metropolitan life has often
been charged with being superficial. And it can

lead to a kind of dispersal, which the great moralists, including Blaise Pascal, warned of. But when wisely practiced it also allows encounters that open us up and awaken our understanding of the diversity of people in the world and their cultures — allowing an enriching human exchange, from which a modern society unquestionably profits.

The extension of our horizon is the third benefit of this book. It opens our eyes to the fact that Expressionist architecture was not only a movement in Germany, but found followers and was taken up by architects in significant parts of Central Europe. Certainly, these were parts of Central Europe where German culture was influential in general. But as always in such cases of cultural linkages, new, aesthetically interesting adaptations emerged: The Swimming Baths in Dachova in Hořice/Horschitz (8) (Czech Republic), the Funereal Chapel and Hall in Turnov/Turnau (11) (Czech Republic), the Housing and Office Building in Obchodná in Bratislava/Pressburg (16) (Slovakia), the Housing in Polička/Politischka (33, 34, 35) (Czech Republic), and the Crematorium in Pardubice/ Pardubitz (37) (Czech Republic) all let their respective local styles shine through, thereby enriching the palette of Expressionist architecture.

For both our historical and aesthetic understanding, this book offers bridges across which our eyes can easily venture, helping the strange become familiar. In a time of a newly awakened narrow-minded nationalism, this publication and its editors help to strengthen a shared vision of a peaceful, open and beautiful Europe.

Gesine Schwan

HEIMAT
METROPOLIS

In einer Zeit, in der vielerorts gegen die
Vielfalt und Multikulturalität der Globalisierung
der Ruf nach »Heimat« erschallt, ist das Buch
»Fragments of Metropolis – Ost« ein besonderes
Geschenk. Zunächst einfach, weil der Band wun-
derbare Fotografien von expressionistischen Bau-
denkmälern zusammenträgt, die schon ästhetisch
eine reine Freude sind. Prächtige Villen, Kirchen,
Synagogen, städtische Wohnhäuser, Kinos, Thea-
ter, Badeanstalten, ja auch Gas- und Wasserwerke
– sie alle strahlen die bunte Vitalität, aber auch die
oft elegante Schönheit des architektonischen Expressionismus aus und bieten uns einen geradezu
sinnlichen Genuss. Es ist einfach ein Vergnügen,
sich diese Bilder anzuschauen.

Aber der Band zeigt auch, dass Heimat
nicht im Gegensatz zu Vielfalt und weltstädtischer
Offenheit stehen muss. Im Gegensatz zu reaktio-
nären, oft regressiven Wünschen, sich in unver-
änderte und möglichst unveränderbare Gehäuse,
die man immer schon kannte, zurückzuziehen
und darin die Heimat »festzuhalten«, lädt dieser
Architekturstil, auch wenn er keineswegs nur in
Großstädten seinen Ausdruck fand, zur Freude am
Experiment und zur Neugier auf ein rauschendes
Leben in der Metropole ein, in der sich die ver-
schiedensten Menschen mit ihren Erfahrungen,
Fantasien und Wünschen treffen. Metropolis ist die
attraktive Alternative zu einer geschlossenen Welt,
deren »Geborgenheit« sich der Langeweile der

steten Wiederkehr des Gleichen und der Konvention verdankt.

Dieses rauschende Metropolenleben ist oft der Oberflächlichkeit bezichtigt worden. Und es kann ja auch in die dauernde Zerstreuung verführen, wovor große Moralisten wie Blaise Pascal immer gewarnt haben. Aber es erlaubt doch, klug praktiziert, auch Begegnungen, die uns öffnen und unser Verständnis für die nun mal bestehende Vielfalt der Menschen auf der Welt und ihrer Kulturen wecken – und die einen bereichernden menschlichen Austausch ermöglichen. Darin liegt der Gewinn für eine moderne Gesellschaft.

Die Erweiterung unseres Horizonts – das ist der dritte Gewinn dieses Buches – öffnet uns überdies die Augen dafür, dass die expressionistische Architektur nicht nur eine Bewegung in Deutschland war, sondern in erheblichen Teilen Zentraleuropas Anhänger und umsetzende Architekten gefunden hat. Sicher, es waren Teile, die durch die deutsche Kultur beeinflusst waren. Aber wie immer in solchen Fällen der kulturellen Verflechtung entstanden neue ästhetisch interessante Anverwandlungen. Die Badeanstalt Dachova in Horschitz/Hořice (8) (Tschechien) etwa, die Trauerhalle in Turnau/Turnov (11) (ebenfalls Tschechien), das Wohn- und Geschäftshaus ›Obchodná‹ in Pressburg/Bratislava (16) (Slowakei), die Wohnhäuser in Politschka/Polička (33, 34, 35) (Tschechien) und das Krematorium in Pardubitz/Pardubice (37) (ebenfalls Tschechien) lassen doch den lokalen Stil durchscheinen, der die expressionistische Architektur bereichert.

Für die allgemeine und für die ästhetische Verständigung bietet das Brücken, über die unser Auge gerne wandert und die dazu beitragen, Fremdes vertraut werden zu lassen. In Zeiten eines neu erwachenden bornierten Nationalismus machen sich der Band und seine Herausgeber damit um ein friedliches, reiches und attraktives Europa verdient.

Beate Störtkuhl

EXPRESSIONISM 'EAST'

The third volume of "Fragments of Metropolis" widens the view beyond the borders of Germany, presenting buildings located in today's Czech Republic, Slovakia and Poland.

The geopolitical contexts of the period in which they were built, between 1905 and 1930, were wholly different: The principal works of the Czech Cubists were built before the First World War, when Bohemia and Moravia belonged to the Austrian half of the Austro-Hungarian Empire, while Slovakia belonged to the Hungarian half. Many of the buildings were built in the Eastern Provinces of the German Reich, which since 1945 have been part of Poland; for instance, the Centennial Hall (136) in Breslau, now Wrocław, which is a prototype of Expressionist architecture. These historical backgrounds are essential for understanding what drove changes in building forms and constructions activities in the respective regions.

"Metropolis East" traces the artistic connections cut off by the Iron Curtain and shows us that we have to look Eastward to make our understanding of European modernism complete. Thus, it becomes very clear that 'Expressionism' is not simply a phenomenon of German and Dutch architectural history: in 1915, Czech 'Cubists' were already proudly writing of the 'assertion of the creative will [...] through expression', a vision also found in the writings of Polish 'Formists'.

Across national borders, artists and architects were engaged in intensive exchange, not only through magazines, but also in personal encounters as part of their involvement in exhibitions or longer study visits. Before the First World War, Der Sturm, Herwarth Walden's Berlin gallery and similarly titled magazine, offered a central forum for Expressionist movements — from Scandinavia to Italy, from France to the then still divided Poland.

But what is Expressionism in architecture? In a work published by Sturm-Verlag in 1915, Adolf Behne (1885–1948), the keen observer and critic of the 'new art' of the early 20th century, formulated one of the first definitions:

'[...] the expressionist architect [...] descends deeply and with great curiosity into the nature of his tasks [...]. For him everything must start from scratch; he creates it all from within. Each form must necessarily be something unique, because the specific conditions of each task will never be the same twice.'

At that time, most of the buildings collected in the three volumes of "Fragments of Metropolis" thus far published were not yet even designed, so whom did Behne have in mind? Certainly two architects from Wrocław in particular, whose works can be found in this book: Hans Poelzig (1869–1936), then director of the local Academy of Arts and Crafts, and the city architect Max Berg (1870–1947). Together they had just designed the exhibition grounds in Wrocław, with its aforementioned centrepiece, the Centennial Hall. For the new construction of a hall for mass events, Max Berg transposed the construction principles of Gothic vaulting to the modern building material of reinforced concrete. At night, the glazed ribbed

Fig. 1
Upper Silesian Tower
at the East German
Exhibition in Poznań
/Posen, Hans Poelzig
1911, contemporary
postcard

dome, 67 metres in diameter, was transformed into a luminous crystal, much like Poelzig's other project of the time for a (now demolished) exhibition tower for the East German exhibition in Poznań /Posen in 1911 (Fig. 1). In a collegial exchange, the two architects materialised Paul Scheerbart's (1863–1915) literary visions and thus inspired Bruno Taut's (1880–1939) subsequent designs of glass architecture.

The Centennial Hall was a sensation at its opening in 1913; in 2006 it was listed by UNESCO as a World Heritage site of modern civil engineering and construction. The ensemble also includes the exhibition pavilion (**see the photographs of 136**) and the parabolic pergola also made in reinforced concrete by Hans Poelzig, who is represented in this volume by three other buildings from his years in Silesia (1900–1916). He gave homely expression to the extension of Gothic town hall (**12**) in Lwówek Śląski/Löwenberg (1903–06) with its deeply drawn tiled roofs borrowed from the regional building tradition. In contrast, his project for an office building (**102**), built 1911–13 on Junkernstrasse in Wrocław, is, in its dynamic rounding at the street corner and its horizontal structure, the prototype of a modern civic architecture — whose influence can be read in buildings such as the Wertheim Department Store (**171**) by Hermann Dernburg (1868–1935), built 15 years later and just a few hundred metres away, or in Erich Mendelsohn's (1887–1953) Weichmann Silk House (**170**) (1922) in Gliwice/ Gleiwitz, Upper Silesia. Of all architects, Behne's characterization of the 'expressionist architect' is most applicable to Poelzig, who did in fact find a unique solution for each project that came to him; only a few others ever achieved comparable plastic modelling of built form. As such, one could say Poelzig is *the* Expressionist architect *avant la lettre*.

In the period before the First World War, the Czech architect Jan Kotěra (1871–1923) (**39, 69, 70, 81, 122**) along with his students Josef Gočár (1880–1945) (**23, 27, 39, 53, 79, 82, 101, 104, 105, 106, 110, 118, 131**), Josef Chochol (1880–1956) (**25, 26, 96, 97**) and Pavel Janák (1882–1956) (**20, 28, 37, 119, 120**) had also developed a sculptural understanding of architecture. The sculpted cornices and crystal-cut faceted pillars of Gočár's House of the Black Madonna (**110**) in Prague (1911–12) make a highly individual attempt to redefine urban architecture. And the crystalline refractions of facades, such as those

of Chochol's multi-family house (96) at Neklanova
56 (1911–13), transferred new ways of seeing developed in cubist and futuristic painting to architecture. At the same time, they made reference to the
Bohemian building tradition, specifically to the
idiosyncratic, expressive buildings of Jan Blažej
(Johann Blasius) Santini-Aichel (1677–1723) (Fig. 2),
which combined the plasticity and liveliness of the
Baroque with the sharp-edged lines of the Gothic.
The architects explicitly understood their exper-
iments in form as a 'New Czech Art' (V. Štech,
1915), setting it apart from to the artistic domi-
nance of Vienna as capital city, and as a manifesto
of national sovereignty. This concept of a 'national
style' was also followed by designs for interiors,
which especially in textiles and wallpapers drew
upon folk art motifs.

 The propositions of the Czech Cubists —
who were present at the Cologne Werkbund Exhibition in 1914 amongst other events — were taken
up in Germany. However, a direct translation of
the facade structures of protruding pointed pillars
and prismatic recessed wall panels as found in the
office building (95) on Agnesstrasse in Wrocław
(1922) by Moritz Hadda (1887–1941) remained the
exception.

 Around the time of the First World War,
the artistic search for spiritual 'depth' and 'expression' was just as much inspired by Wassily
Kandinsky's (1866–1944) work "Concerning the
Spiritual" in Art (1911) and the Gothic reception of
the art historian Wilhelm Worringer (1881–1965).
His book "Abstraction and Empathy", which first
appeared in 1907, became a bestseller not least
because it interpreted artistic phenomena in terms
of so-called folk psychology (Völkerpsychologie),
thus providing cultural arguments for national

Fig. 2
Pilgrimage Church of
Saint John of Nepo-
muk in Zelená Hora,
Jan Blažej (Johann
Blasius) Santini-
Aichel, 1719–22

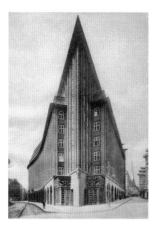

emancipation movements at the time. To Worringer, Gothic was the highest achievement of the spiritualized — 'abstract' — artistic desire of 'Nordic man', a term that could apply just as much to the Czechs as to the Germans, Scandinavians or Poles. Even though the author himself contradicted such interpretations, Worringer's texts were used by others to locate the different Expressionist tendencies in idealistic and — especially in the time of upheaval after 1918 — national traditions.

      The golden age of Expressionist projects began after the First World War. Many designs were for utopian settings for a new society or community that people longed for after the period of political upheaval — such as the fantastic 'City Crowns' and crystal towers that Bruno Taut and his colleagues at the 'Glass Chain' developed while they struggled for real commissions in the economic hardship of the first few years after the war. And initially pragmatic concepts, such as a ring of office towers that Max Berg designed for Wrocław in order to reclaim misused living spaces, were too monumental to be realized. Widely published and discussed, the crystalline, steeply rising shapes of the designs made between 1917 and 1921 nevertheless exerted a strong influence on building at that time. This can be seen, for example, in the Chile House (1922–24) in Hamburg, a brick 'skyscraper' (Fig. 3) that became a symbol of German re-emergence after the war and an exemplary building for an Expressionism understood as 'national style'. Its architect, Fritz Höger (1877–1949), appealed to the history of the medieval Hanseatic League and the spread of 'German' Gothic up to the Baltic region, in order to romanticise brick as a 'Germanic-Nordic' building material. More brick towers, in the form of a monumentally understood

Fig. 3
Chile House in Hamburg, Fritz Höger, 1922–24, contemporary image

Gleiwitz. Eichendorff-Oberlyzeum.

'modernised Gothic', emerged in the French-occupied Rhineland and in the capital, Berlin. They are gathered in the first two volumes of "Fragments of Metropolis".

The present volume shows that this architectural style was also well received in the then German eastern provinces — Silesia, Pomerania, Posen-West Prussia, East Prussia — and in the Free City of Danzig, which were particularly affected by the territorial relinquishment that came as a consequence of the war. From the 'modernized Gothic', a cultural lineage was drawn back to medieval architecture in the context of 'German colonization of the East' to underline contemporary claims of territorial ownership.

In the Upper Silesian border towns of Bytom/Beuthen, Gliwice/Gleiwitz and Zabrze/Hindenburg, the new repertoire of forms was quickly adopted, for instance in the elegant and sophisticated Hotel Admiral Palast (91) in Zabrze (1924–28) by Richard Bielenberg (1871–1929) and Josef Moser (biographical data unknown), which brought a little big-city flair to the industrial agglomeration that had just been raised to the status of a city.

The commission for the urban design was awarded to Dominikus Böhm from Cologne, the star architect of the time. In light of the economic situation, his plans for Zabrze remained fragmentary; however, St Joseph's Church (161) was realized with a monumental, open arcade wall.

Many ambitious projects failed to come to fruition, such as the city hall designs of the Gliwice city councillor Karl Schabik (1882–1945), a high-rise complex with Gothic details (1924–25), reminiscent of Bruno Taut's 'City Crowns'. The fascinating effect of the steeply rising 'bow' of the

Fig. 4
Eichendorff Secondary School in Gliwice/Gleiwitz, Karl Schabik, 1928–30, contemporary postcard

Chile House can still be seen in the late 1920s, when Schabik took up the triangular motif at the Eichendorff Secondary School (142) in Gliwice (Fig. 4), which today belongs to the Silesian University of Technology. The charged symbolism of the forms made them particularly suitable for school buildings, which were perceived, in the language of those days, as 'strongholds of the German cultural treasure in the frontier march'.

Beyond such political connotations, the decorative value of triangular figures, pointed crowns and Gothic figures carved into doorways and walls was appreciated in private houses as well as in public building projects. The lobby of the main hall (Fig. 5) of the train station in Legnica/Liegnitz is impressive with its turquoise and black-green ceramic tiles, crystalline ornaments and dynamic, round counter tables. Here, the transition between Expressionism and Art Deco became fluid.

The Gothic mysticism of light and the aesthetics of crystalline fragmentation also fascinated the Polish Expressionists, who had come together before the First World War in Kraków as 'Formiści' (Formists) and in Poznań as the group 'Bunt' (Rebellion).

The Vistula Gothic style and the folk art of the Polish mountain regions provided the models for the folkloristic-expressive 'Polish decorative art' of the interwar period, which, as a variant of Art Deco, functioned as a 'national style', particularly in interior design and handicraft. At the Exposition Internationale des Arts Décoratifs et Industriels Modernes in Paris in 1925 (Fig. 6), as well as at the National State Exhibition in Poznań, held to celebrate the tenth anniversary of the state, the new Poland presented itself through ephemeral

Fig. 5
Ticket Hall of the Station in Legnica/Liegnitz, Reichsbahndirektion Breslau, 1922–29

Fig. 6
Polish Pavilion at the Exposition Internationale des Arts Décoratifs et Industriels Modernes in Paris, Józef Czajkowski, 1925, contemporary image

glass pavilions. They are reminiscent of the crystalline visions of German Expressionists and reflect the close artistic connections beyond interstate antagonisms. Even today, one is impressed by the experience of the combination of Expressionist glass architecture and elements of folk art in the School of Economics (**126, 127, 128**) in Warsaw, built from 1925 on by Jan Witkiewicz (1881–1958).

In the newly founded Czechoslovak Republic in 1918, Josef Gočár and Pavel Janák replaced the sharp articulations of the facades with plastically rounded elements and decorations (**e.g. 37, 118, 119**). The architects also understood this so-called Rondocubism to be a 'national' architectural style, which was intended to give expression to the long-awaited state sovereignty. Construction in the Slovak part of the country, which was closely connected to the Hungarian architectural scene before 1918 (**e.g. 10**), was now based on Czech models. For example, the residential and commercial building at the Obchodná (**16**) in Bratislava/Pressburg (1924) by Jindřich Merganc (biographical data unknown) continued the cubist, sharp-edged segmentation of facades. In contrast, Klement Šilinger (1887–1951), who took over Merganc's projects, followed Rondocubist design principles, as can be seen in his project for the Commercial School (**36**) in Neutra/Nitra (1922–26).

Rondocubism remained a short episode; its Prague protagonists themselves soon found the decorative applications unsatisfactory, veiling the constructive core of the buildings. They incorporated contemporary discourse on the functional orientation of architecture – the geometric, ornament-free forms of modernism prevailed in the state architecture from the mid-1920s onward – as symbols of a modern, progressive Czechoslovakia.

In Germany as well, the 'Neues Bauen' ('New Building') questioned the massive plasticity and the joy of ornament found in Expressionist form-finding. Unlike in Czechoslovakia, it was the state building departments of the postal service, railway and the judiciary in particular, which even up until the late 1920s were proudly building new examples of 'modernised brick Gothic'. The Police Headquarters (**133**) in Wrocław (1925–27) and the Police Prison (**72**) in Legnica (1929–30) have the effect, in terms of an *architecture parlante*, of inducing respect or even fear. The Postal Cheque Office (**133**) in Breslau, by the postal service's chief architect Lothar Neumann (1926–29), the city's first 'skyscraper' with slender, angular, towering murals and a jagged parapet, was a late and reduced version of the tower designs by Max Berg.

Looking back today, the architectural infighting of the 1920s is only an interesting historical phenomenon. The sculptural forms and decorative qualities of Expressionist architecture exert their very own kind of fascination. In the photographs of the buildings presented in this volume — all of which were sculpturally conceived — an aesthetic spectrum resulting from the various factors relating to specific chronologies, groups and individuals can be traced and appreciated.

Quoted contemporary literature

Behne, Adolf: Zur neuen Kunst. Berlin 1915.

Gočár, Josef; Janák, Pavel; Kysela, František: Čechische Bestrebungen um ein modernes Interieur. Mit einer Einleitung von Dr. V. V. Štech. Prague 1915.

Höger, Fritz: Der neue deutsche Baustil, in: Deutsche Bauzeitung 63 (1929), p. 575.

Kandinsky, Wassili: Über das Geistige in der Kunst. Munich 1911.

Worringer, Wilhelm: Abstraktion und Einfühlung. Ein Beitrag zur Stilpsychologie. Neuwied 1907.

Beate Störtkuhl

EXPRESSIONISMUS »OST«

Der dritte Band der »Fragments of Metropolis« weitet den Blick über die Grenzen der Bun-
desrepublik Deutschland hinaus. Die hier präsen-
tierten Bauten stehen im heutigen Tschechien, in
der Slowakei und in Polen.

Die geopolitischen Kontexte ihrer Entste-
hungszeit zwischen 1905 und 1930 waren gänzlich
verschieden: Die Hauptwerke der tschechischen
Kubisten entstanden vor dem Ersten Weltkrieg, als
Böhmen und Mähren dem österreichischen Teil
der K.-u.-k.-Monarchie angehörten, während die
Slowakei Teil der ungarischen Reichshälfte war.
Viele Objekte wurden in den damaligen Ostprovinzen des Deutschen Reiches errichtet, die seit
1945 zu Polen gehören; etwa die Jahrhunderthalle (136) im schlesischen Breslau, dem heutigen
Wrocław, ein Prototyp expressionistischen Bauens.
Diese historischen Hintergründe sind wesentlich
für das Verständnis von Baukonjunkturen und
Baugestaltungen in den jeweiligen Regionen.

»Metropolis Ost« spürt den durch den
»Eisernen Vorhang« gekappten künstlerischen
Verbindungen nach und führt uns vor Augen, dass
das Bild der europäischen Moderne erst durch den
Blick nach Osten komplett wird. Dabei wird sehr
deutlich, dass »Expressionismus« kein Phänomen
der deutschen und niederländischen Architektur-
geschichte ist: Die »Geltendmachung des schöpfe-
rischen Willens [...] durch den Ausdruck« schrie-
ben sich die tschechischen »Kubisten« bereits 1915

auf die Fahnen, ganz ähnlich formulierten auch
die polnischen »Formisten«.

Über Ländergrenzen hinweg standen
Künstler und Architekten in einem intensiven Austausch, nicht nur über Zeitschriften, sondern auch
in persönlichen Begegnungen im Rahmen von
Ausstellungsbeteiligungen oder längeren Studien-
aufenthalten. Ein zentrales Forum für expressionistische Strömungen – von Skandinavien bis Italien,
von Frankreich bis in das damals noch geteilte
Polen – boten vor dem Ersten Weltkrieg Herwarth
Waldens Berliner Galerie Der Sturm und seine
gleichnamige Zeitschrift.

Was aber ist eigentlich Expressionismus
in der Architektur? In einer Publikation des
Sturm-Verlags formulierte 1915 Adolf Behne
(1885–1948), der seismografische Begleiter und
Kritiker der »neuen Kunst« des frühen 20. Jahrhunderts, eine der ersten Definitionen:

»[...] der expressionistische Architekt [...]
steigt in das Wesen seiner Aufgaben ganz tief und
ganz gespannt hinab [...]. Ihm ergibt sich alles aufs
neue vom Grund aus, er schafft ganz von innen.
Notwendig ist ihm jede Form etwas Einmaliges,
weil niemals bei einer neuen Aufgabe genau die
gleichen Bedingungen wiederkehren können.«

Die meisten der in den mittlerweile drei
Bänden der »Fragments of Metropolis« versam-
melten Bauten waren zu diesem Zeitpunkt noch
nicht einmal in Planung. Wen also hatte Behne mit
seiner Charakterisierung im Sinn? Sicherlich auch
zwei Architekten aus Breslau, deren Werke sich
in diesem Buch finden: Hans Poelzig (1869–1936),
den damaligen Direktor der dortigen Akademie
für Kunst und Kunstgewerbe, sowie den Stadtbau-
rat Max Berg (1870–1947). Gemeinsam hatten sie
gerade das Breslauer Messegelände mit der schon

Abb. 1
Oberschlesischer
Turm auf der Ost-
deutschen Ausstellung
in Posen/Poznań,
Hans Poelzig, 1911,
zeitgenössische
Postkarte

erwähnten Jahrhunderthalle konzipiert. Für die neue Bauaufgabe einer Halle für Massenveranstaltungen transponierte Max Berg die Konstruktionsprinzipien gotischer Strebewerke in den modernen Baustoff Eisenbeton. Die verglaste Rippenkuppel mit einem Durchmesser von 67 Metern verwandelte sich bei nächtlicher Illumination in einen leuchtenden Kristall, ähnlich wie Poelzigs gleichzeitig entstandener (nicht erhaltener) Ausstellungsturm für die Ostdeutsche Ausstellung in Posen/Poznań 1911 (Abb. 1). Im kollegialen Austausch materialisierten die beiden Architekten Paul Scheerbarts (1863–1915) literarische Visionen und inspirierten damit auch die darauffolgenden Entwürfe einer gläsernen Baukunst von Bruno Taut (1880–1939).

Die Jahrhunderthalle war bei ihrer Eröffnung 1913 eine Sensation; 2006 wurde sie als Schlüsselwerk moderner Bau- und Ingenieurskunst in die Liste des UNESCO-Weltkulturerbes eingetragen. Zum Ensemble gehören auch der Ausstellungspavillon (siehe Fotografie zu 136) und die parabolische Pergola, ebenfalls aus armiertem Beton, von Hans Poelzig, der im vorliegenden Band mit drei weiteren Bauten aus seinen Jahren in Schlesien (1900–1916) vertreten ist. Dem Anbau des gotischen Rathauses (12) in Löwenberg/Lwówek Śląski (1903–06) verlieh er mit tief herabgezogenen, der regionalen Bautradition entlehnten Ziegeldächern einen anheimelnden Ausdruck. Dagegen ist sein 1911–13 erbautes Geschäftshaus (102) an der Breslauer Junkernstraße mit der dynamischen Verschleifung der Straßenecke und der horizontalen Gliederung der Prototyp moderner Großstadtarchitektur – ablesbar unter anderem am fünfzehn Jahre später entstandenen, nur wenige hundert Meter entfernten Warenhaus Wertheim (171) von Hermann Dernburg (1868–1935) oder an Erich Mendelsohns (1887–1953) Seidenhaus Weichmann (170) (1922) im oberschlesischen Gleiwitz/Gliwice. Auf kaum einen Architekten trifft Behnes Charakterisierung des »expressionistischen Architekten« mehr zu als auf Poelzig, der tatsächlich für jede Bauaufgabe eine individuelle Lösung fand; nur wenige erreichen eine vergleichbar plastische Modellierung der Bauformen – Poelzig ist *der* expressionistische Architekt *avant la lettre*.

Ein skulpturales Verständnis von Architektur entwickelten vor dem Ersten Weltkrieg auch die tschechischen Architekten Jan Kotěra (1871–1923) (39, 69, 70, 81, 122) und seine Schüler

Josef Gočár (1880–1945) (23, 27, 39, 53, 79, 82, 101, 104,
105, 106, 110, 118, 131), Josef Chochol (1880–1956)
(25, 26, 96, 97) und Pavel Janák (1882–1956) (20, 28,
37, 119, 120). Plastisch herausgearbeitete Gesimse
und kristallin geschnittene Stützen machen
Gočárs Haus zur Schwarzen Muttergottes (110)
in Prag (1911–12) zu einem höchst individuellen
Versuch, Großstadtarchitektur neu zu definie-
ren. Die kristallinen Brechungen der Fassaden,
etwa an Chochols Prager Mehrfamilienhaus (96)
(1911–13), übertrugen neue Sehweisen der kubistischen und futuristischen Malerei auf die Architektur. Zugleich nahmen sie Bezug auf die böhmi-
sche Bautradition, konkret auf die eigenwilligen,
expressiven Bauten des Jan Blažej (Johann Blasius)
Santini-Aichel (1677–1723) (Abb. 2), der Plastizität
und Bewegtheit des Barock mit den scharfkantigen
Linien der Gotik verband. Ihre Formgebungen verstanden die Architekten explizit als »neue čechische Kunst« (V. Štech, 1915), in Abgrenzung zur
künstlerischen Dominanz der Hauptstadt Wien
und als Manifest nationaler Souveränität. Diesem
Konzept eines »Nationalstils« folgten auch die
Entwürfe für Interieurs, die vor allem für Textilien
und Tapeten Motive aus der Volkskunst aufgriffen.

    Die Anregungen der tschechischen Kubis-
ten, die unter anderem auf der Kölner Werkbund-
ausstellung 1914 präsent waren, wurden auch in
Deutschland aufgenommen. Eine direkte Über-
nahme der Fassadenstrukturen aus spitz hervor-
tretenden Pfeilern und prismenförmig vertieften
Wandfeldern wie am Bürohaus (95) an der Breslauer Agnesstraße (1922) von Moritz Hadda (1887–
1941) blieb allerdings die Ausnahme.

    Die künstlerische Suche nach geistiger
»Tiefe« und »Ausdruck« war in den Jahren um den
Ersten Weltkrieg gleichermaßen inspiriert von

Abb. 2
Wallfahrtskirche
Hl. Johannes Nepo-
muk in Grüneberg/
Zelená Hora, Jan
Blažej (Johann
Blasius) Santini-
Aichel, 1719–22

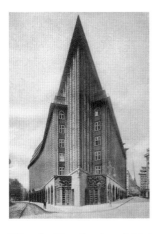

Wassily Kandinskys (1866–1944) Schrift »Über
das Geistige in der Kunst« (1911) und der Gotik-
Rezeption des Kunsthistorikers Wilhelm Worringer
(1881–1965). Dessen erstmals 1907 erschienenes
Buch »Abstraktion und Einfühlung« wurde nicht
zuletzt deshalb zu einem Bestseller, weil er darin
künstlerische Phänomene völkerpsychologisch
deutete und damit den zeitgenössischen nationalen
Emanzipationsbestrebungen kulturelle Argumente
lieferte. Die Gotik galt ihm als höchste Errungen-
schaft des vergeistigten – »abstrakten« – Kunst-
wollens des »nordischen Menschen«. Von dieser
Formulierung konnten sich Tschechen ebenso
angesprochen fühlen wie Deutsche, Skandinavier
oder Polen. Auch wenn der Autor selbst derartigen
Auslegungen widersprach, wurden Worringers
Texte herangezogen, um die unterschiedlichen expressionistischen Strömungen in eine ideelle und
– insbesondere in der Umbruchzeit nach 1918 –
nationale Traditionslinie zu stellen.

    Die Hochzeit expressionistischer Projekte
begann nach dem Ersten Weltkrieg. Nicht wenige
Entwürfe zeigten utopische Gehäuse einer neuen
Gesellschaft bzw. Gemeinschaft, deren Formie-
rung man nach den politischen Umbrüchen er-
hoffte, so etwa die fantastischen »Stadtkronen«
und Kristalltürme, die Bruno Taut und seine Kol-
legen der »Gläsernen Kette« entwickelten, während sie in der wirtschaftlichen Not der ersten
Nachkriegsjahre um reale Aufträge kämpften.
Und auch zunächst pragmatisch wirkende Kon-
zepte wie der Ring von Geschäftshochhäusern,
den Max Berg für Breslau konzipierte, um zweck-
entfremdeten Wohnraum zurückzugewinnen,
waren zu monumental gedacht, um realisiert werden zu können. Vielfach publiziert und diskutiert,
übten die kristallinen, steil aufragenden Formen

Abb. 3
Chilehaus in Ham-
burg, Fritz Höger
1922–24, zeitgenössi-
sche Abbildung

der zwischen 1917 und 1921 entstandenen Entwürfe dennoch einen starken Einfluss auf das Bauen
aus. Dies lässt sich etwa am Hamburger Chilehaus
(1922–24) (Abb. 3) ablesen, einem »Hochhaus« aus
Backstein, das zum Symbol des deutschen Wiederaufstiegs nach dem Krieg und zum Referenzbau
eines als »Nationalstil« verstandenen Expressionismus wurde. Sein Architekt Fritz Höger (1877–
1949) rekurrierte auf die mittelalterliche Hanse
und die Ausbreitung der »deutschen« Gotik bis in
den Ostseeraum, um den Backstein als »germanisch-nordischen« Baustoff zu verklären. Weitere
Backsteinhochhäuser in den Formen einer monumental verstandenen »modernisierten Gotik«
entstanden im französisch besetzten Rheinland
sowie in der Hauptstadt Berlin – sie sind versammelt in den beiden ersten Bänden der »Fragments
of Metropolis«.

Der vorliegende Band zeigt, dass dieser Architekturduktus auch in den damaligen
deutschen Ostprovinzen – Schlesien, Pommern,
Grenzmark Posen-Westpreußen, Ostpreußen –
und in der Freien Stadt Danzig, die durch Gebietsabtretungen von den Kriegsfolgen besonders
betroffen waren, großen Zuspruch fand. Von der
»modernisierten Gotik« wurde eine kulturelle
Traditionslinie zur mittelalterlichen Baukunst im
Kontext der »deutschen Ostkolonisation« gezogen, um aktuelle territoriale Besitzansprüche zu
unterstreichen.

In den oberschlesischen Grenzstädten
Beuthen/Bytom, Gleiwitz/Gliwice und Hindenburg/Zabrze wurde das neue Formenrepertoire
rasch aufgegriffen, etwa im elegant-mondänen
Hotel Admiralspalast (91) in Hindenburg (1924–
28) von Richard Bielenberg (1871–1929) und Josef
Moser (Lebensdaten unbekannt), das ein wenig

Abb. 4
Eichendorff-Gymnasium in Gleiwitz/
Gliwice, Karl
Schabik, 1928–30,
zeitgenössische
Postkarte

Großstadtflair in die eben erst zur Stadt erhobene Industrieagglomeration brachte.

Mit der urbanen Strukturierung wurde der damalige »Stararchitekt« Dominikus Böhm aus Köln beauftragt. Angesichts der Wirtschaftslage blieben seine Planungen für Hindenburg Stückwerk; realisiert wurde die St.-Josephs-Kirche (161) mit einer monumentalen, offenen Arkadenwand.

Viele ambitionierte Projekte scheiterten, etwa die Rathausentwürfe des Gleiwitzer Stadtbaurats Karl Schabik (1882–1945), ein Hochhauskomplex mit gotisierenden Details (1924–25), die an Bruno Tauts »Stadtkronen« erinnern. Die Faszination, die der steil aufragende »Bug« des Chilehauses ausübte, zeigt sich noch Ende der 1920er-Jahre, als Schabik das Dreiecksmotiv beim Gleiwitzer Eichendorff-Gymnasium (142) (Abb. 4) (heute ein Teil der Technischen Universität) aufgriff. Die symbolische Aufladung der Formen machte sie besonders geeignet für Schulbauten, den – im zeitgenössischen Duktus – »Trutzburg[en] deutschen Kulturschatzes in der Grenzmark«.

Jenseits solcher politischen Konnotationen wurde der dekorative Wert der Dreiecksfiguren, Zackenkronen und der gotischen Skulpturen nachempfundenen Konsolfiguren an Portalen und Wänden geschätzt, im privaten Wohnungsbau ebenso wie bei öffentlichen Bauvorhaben. Beeindruckend ist die Schalterhalle des Bahnhofs in Liegnitz/Legnica (Abb. 5) mit türkisen und schwarzgrünen Keramikkacheln, kristallinen Ornamenten und dynamisch gerundeten Schaltertischen – die Übergänge zwischen Expressionismus und Art Déco wurden fließend.

Die aus der Gotik abgeleitete Lichtmystik und die Ästhetik der kristallinen Splitterung

Abb. 5
Schalterhalle des Bahnhofs in Liegnitz/ Legnica, Reichsbahndirektion Breslau, 1922–29

Abb. 6
Polnischer Pavillon auf der Exposition Internationale des Arts Décoratifs et Industriels Modernes in Paris, Józef Czajkowski, 1925, zeitgenössische Fotografie

faszinierten auch die polnischen Expressionisten, die sich vor dem Ersten Weltkrieg in Krakau als »Formiści« (Formisten), in Posen als Gruppe »Bunt« (Aufruhr) zusammengefunden hatten.

Die »Weichselgotik« und die Volkskunst der polnischen Gebirgsregionen lieferten die Vorbilder für die folkloristisch-expressive »polnische Dekorationskunst« der Zwischenkriegszeit, die als Variante des Art Déco insbesondere in der Raumgestaltung und im Kunsthandwerk als »Nationalstil« funktionierte. Sowohl auf der Exposition Internationale des Arts Décoratifs et Industriels Modernes in Paris 1925 als auch auf der Allgemeinen Landesausstellung in Posen zum zehnjährigen Staatsjubiläum präsentierte sich das neue Polen in ephemeren Glaspavillons (Abb. 6). Sie erinnern an die kristallinen Visionen deutscher Expressionisten und spiegeln die engen künstlerischen Verflechtungen jenseits der zwischenstaatlichen Antagonismen wider. Eindrucksvoll lässt sich jene Verbindung von expressionistischer Glasarchitektur und Elementen der Volkskunst noch heute in der ab 1925 erbauten Höheren Handelsschule (126, 127, 128) in Warschau/Warszawa von Jan Witkiewicz (1881–1958) erleben.

In der 1918 neu gegründeten Tschechoslowakischen Republik ersetzten Josef Gočár und Pavel Janák die kantigen Splitterungen der Fassaden durch plastisch gerundete Gliederungselemente und Dekors (z.B. 37, 118, 119). Auch diesen sogenannten Rondokubismus verstanden die Architekten als »nationalen« Baustil, welcher der lang ersehnten staatlichen Souveränität Ausdruck verleihen sollte. Das Baugeschehen im slowakischen Landesteil, das vor 1918 eng mit der ungarischen Architekturszene verbunden war (z.B. 10), orientierte sich nun an tschechischen Vorbildern. Ganz der kubistischen, scharfgratigen Segmentierung der Fassaden folgt beispielsweise das Wohn- und Geschäftshaus an der Obchodná (16) in Pressburg/ Bratislava (1924) von Jindřich Merganc (Lebensdaten unbekannt). Dagegen übernahm Klement Šilinger (1887–1951) in seinen Projekten, etwa für die Handelsschule (36) in Neutra/Nitra (1922–26), die rondokubistischen Gestaltungsprinzipien.

Der Rondokubismus blieb eine kurze Episode; seine Prager Protagonisten selbst befanden die dekorativen Applikationen bald als unbefriedigend, den konstruktiven Kern des Baus verschleiernd. Sie griffen die aktuellen Diskurse zur Versachlichung und Funktionsorientiertheit der Architektur auf – die geometrischen, ornamentlosen Formen des Neuen Bauens setzten sich ab Mitte der 1920er-Jahre auch in der staatlichen Repräsentationsarchitektur durch – als Symbole einer modernen, fortschrittsorientierten Tschechoslowakei.

Auch in Deutschland stellte das Neue Bauen die wuchtige Plastizität und die Dekorfreude expressionistischer Formfindungen infrage. Anders als in der Tschechoslowakei waren es hier insbesondere die staatlichen Bauverwaltungen von Post, Bahn und Justiz, die bis in die späten 1920er-Jahre an den auftrumpfenden Formen einer »modernisierten Backsteingotik« festhielten. Das Polizeipräsidium (133) in Breslau (1925–27) oder der Gefängnisbau (72) in Liegnitz (1929–30) wirken im Sinne einer *architecture parlante* respekt- oder gar furchteinflößend. Das Breslauer Postscheckamt (135) des Post-Baumeisters Lothar Neumann (1926–29), das erste »Hochhaus« der Stadt mit schlanken, kantigen, steil aufragenden Wandvorlagen und einer gezackten Attika, ist eine späte und reduzierte Umsetzung der Hochhausentwürfe Max Bergs.

Aus der heutigen Distanz sind die architektonischen Richtungskämpfe der 1920er-Jahre nur noch ein interessantes historisches Phänomen. Die plastische Durchformung und die dekorativen Qualitäten expressionistischer Baukunst üben eine ganz eigene Faszination aus. Chronologische, gruppenspezifische und künstlerisch-individuelle Faktoren führten zu einer ästhetischen Bandbreite, die sich hier in den Fotografien der stets skulptural gedachten Objekte nachverfolgen und genießen lässt.

Zitierte zeitgenössische Literatur

Behne, Adolf: Zur neuen Kunst. Berlin 1915.

Gočár, Josef; Janák, Pavel; Kysela, František: Čechische Bestrebungen um ein modernes Interieur. Mit einer Einleitung von Dr. V. V. Štech. Prag 1915.

Höger, Fritz: Der neue deutsche Baustil, in: Deutsche Bauzeitung 63 (1929), S. 575.

Kandinsky, Wassili: Über das Geistige in der Kunst. München 1911.

Worringer, Wilhelm: Abstraktion und Einfühlung. Ein Beitrag zur Stilpsychologie. Neuwied 1907.

THE FRAGMENTS
DIE FRAGMENTE

And this pulsating, soaring vitality of
line and mass is truly what is called
Expressionism.

Marlene Moeschke-Poelzig, letter to
Hans Poelzig, 1918

Und dieses Schwingen, Steigen, Leben-
digsein der Linien und Massen ist wirklich
doch, was man Expressionismus nennt.

Marlene Moeschke-Poelzig, Brief an
Hans Poelzig, 1918

1

Street Lamp | Straßenlaterne, Jungmannovo náměstí, Prague | Prag |
Praha, Czech Republic | Tschechien (J), Emil Králíček, 1912–13

2
Milk House | Milchhaus, Plac Konstytucji 3 Maja, Głogów | Glogau,
Poland | Polen (A), Erwin Griesinger, 1926?–28?

3
House of the Society for Natural Living and Medicine | Haus des
Vereins für naturgemäße Lebens- und Heilweise, Wojciecha z
Brudzewa 8, Wrocław | Breslau, Poland | Polen (D), Max Taubert,
1929

4

František Bílek's Studio and House | Atelier- und Wohnhaus František
Bílek, Mickiewiczova 233/1, Prague | Prag | Praha, Czech Republic |
Tschechien (J), František Bílek, Antonín Hulán, 1910–11

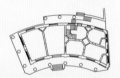

4
František Bílek's Studio and House | Atelier- und Wohnhaus František Bílek, Mickiewiczova 233/1, Prague | Prag | Praha, Czech Republic | Tschechien (J), František Bílek, Antonín Hulán, 1910–11

5
Villa Benies | Villa Benies, Mírová 147, Lysá nad Labem | Lissa an der
Elbe, Czech Republic | Tschechien (B), Emil Králíček, 1912–13

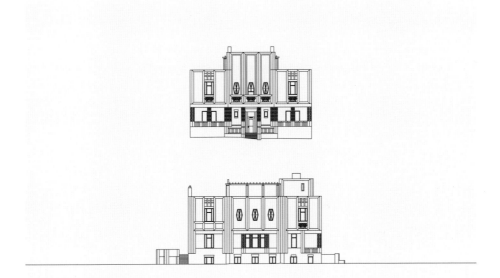

0   20

5
Villa Benies | Villa Benies, Mírová 147, Lysá nad Labem | Lissa an der
Elbe, Czech Republic | Tschechien (B), Emil Králíček, 1912–13

6

Adam Żeromski Mausoleum | Mausoleum Adam Żeromski, Stefana
Żeromskiego 8, Nałęczów, Poland | Polen (A), Jan Witkiewicz
[Koszczyc], 1920–22

7

Tyrš Lookout Tower | Aussichtsturm Tyrš, Na Rozarce, Žamberka,
Czech Republic | Tschechien (B), Theodor Petřík, 1932

8

Dachova Swimming Baths | Badeanstalt Dachova, Dachova 463,
Hořice | Horschitz, Czech Republic | Tschechien (B), Karel Bachura,
1925

9

Villa Vondrák | Villa Vondrák, Západní 488/21, Prague | Prag | Praha,
Czech Republic | Tschechien (J), Jaroslav Vondrák, 1923–24

10
Primary School | Grundschule, Lichardova 140/4, Skalica | Skalitz,
Slovakia | Slowakei (B), Józef Bábolnay, 1913

11
Funeral Chapel | Trauerhalle, Přemyslova, Turnov | Turnau, Czech
Republic | Tschechien (B), Vladimír Krýš

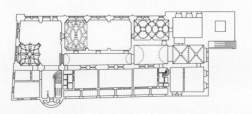

Extension, Town Hall | Erweiterung Rathaus, Plac Wolności, Lwówek
Śląski | Löwenberg, Poland | Polen (A), Hans Poelzig, 1903–06

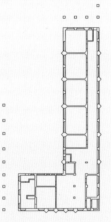

0   20

13
School for Military Families | Schule der Militärfamilien, Stefana
Czarnieckiego 49, Warsaw | Warschau | Warszawa, Poland | Polen (E),
Jan Witkiewicz [Koszczyc], 1930–34

Conversion, Villa Františky Lipčíkové | Umbau Villa Františky
Lipčíkové, Brněnská 500/80, Olomouc | Olmütz, Czech Republic |
Tschechien (B), Rudolf Stockar, 1918–19

15
Station | Bahnhof, Plac Dworcowy, Zbąszynek | Neu Bentschen,
Poland | Polen (A), Wilhelm Beringer, ca. 1925

16

Flats and Shops | Wohn- und Geschäftshaus, Obchodná 528/48,
Bratislava | Pressburg, Slovakia | Slowakei (L), Jindřich Merganc, 1924

17
Offices, F.J. Materna Factory | Verwaltungsgebäude Fabrik F.J.
Materna , Dělnická 313/20, Prague | Prag | Praha, Czech Republic |
Tschechien (J), Rudolf Stockar, 1919?–20

18

Factory | Fabrikgebäude, Nádražní 889, Přelouč | Prelauc, Czech
Republic | Tschechien (B), frühe 1920er? | early 1920s?

19
Flats | Wohnhaus, Ľadová 3077/10, Bratislava | Pressburg, Slovakia |
Slowakei (L), Klement Šilinger, ca. 1923

20

Villa Drechsel | Villa Drechsel, Strachovská 331, Pelhřimov |
Pilgrams, Czech Republic | Tschechien (B), Pavel Janák, 1912–13

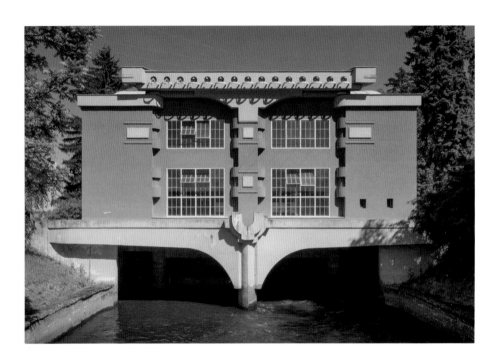

Plhák Brothers Water Power Station | Wasserkraftwerk Gebrüder
Plhák, Úsov 71, Třeština | Trittschein, Czech Republic | Tschechien (B),
Josef Štěpánek, 1921

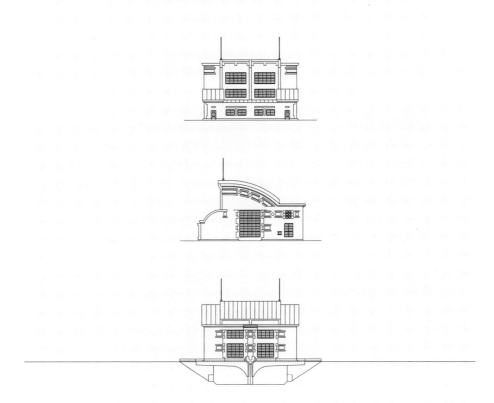

22

Villa Plhák Brothers (Villa Háj) | Villa Gebrüder Plhák (Villa Háj),
Úsov 71, Třeština | Trittschein, Czech Republic | Tschechien (B),
Bohuslav Fuchs, 1921

23
Villa Bauer | Villa Bauer, Libodřice 111, Libodřice, Czech Republic |
Tschechien (B), Josef Gočár, 1912–14

0   20

Municipal Cinema (Hvězda Cinema) | Stadtkino (Kino Hvězda),
Osvobození 776, Kamenický Šenov | Steinschönau, Czech Republic |
Tschechien (B), Leo Kammel, 1927?

25
Villa Kovařovic | Villa Kovařovic, Libušina 49/3, Prague | Prag |
Praha, Czech Republic | Tschechien (J), Josef Chochol, 1912–13

25
Villa Kovařovic | Villa Kovařovic, Libušina 49/3, Prague | Prag |
Praha, Czech Republic | Tschechien (J), Josef Chochol, 1912–13

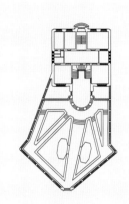

0   20

Triplex House | Dreifamilienhaus, Rašínovo nábřeží 42/6–10, Prague |
Prag | Praha, Czech Republic | Tschechien (J), Josef Chochol, 1912–13

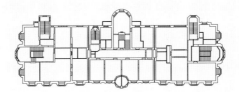

27

Stach and Hoffmann Detached Houses | Einfamilienhäuser Stach
und Hoffmann, Tychonova 269/4–6, Prague | Prag | Praha, Czech
Republic | Tschechien (J), Josef Gočár, 1912–13

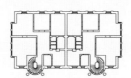

28

Conversion, Fára House | Umbau Haus Fára, Masarykovo náměstí 13,
Pelhřimov | Pilgrams, Czech Republic | Tschechien (B), Pavel Janák,
1913?

29
Synagogue | Synagoge, Sokolovská 209/9, Milevsko | Mühlhausen,
Czech Republic | Tschechien (B), Oldřich Tyl, 1914–19

Flats of Václva Rejchla, Senior | Wohnhaus Václva Rejchla senior,
Československé armády 556/31, Hradec Králové | Königgrätz, Czech
Republic | Tschechien (K), Bohumil Waigant, 1914

31

Flats of Joseph Jihlavec | Wohnhaus Joseph Jihlavec, Československé
armády 543/29, Hradec Králové | Königgrätz, Czech Republic |
Tschechien (K), Bohumil Waigant, 1913

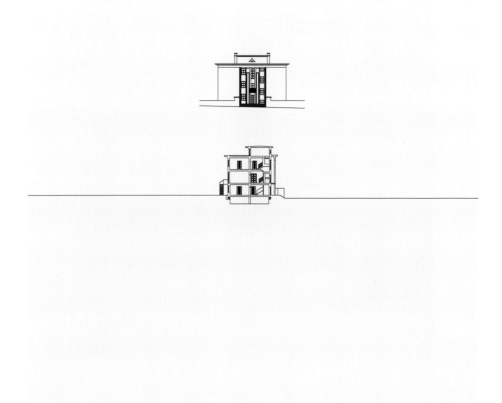

32
Villa Tadeusz Michejda | Villa Tadeusz Michejda, Księcia Józefa
Poniatowskiego 19, Katowice | Kattowitz, Poland | Polen (B), Tadeusz
Michejda, 1926

33

Flats | Wohnhäuser, Edvarda Beneše 389–391, Rumunská 39,
Československé armády 388, Polička | Politschka, Czech Republic |
Tschechien (B), Václav Flegl, 1923–24

34
Flats | Wohnhäuser, Rumunská 410–411, Polička | Politschka, Czech
Republic | Tschechien (B), Václav Flegl?, 1922–24

35
Flats | Wohnhäuser, Nábřeží svobody 384–386, 393, Polička |
Politschka, Czech Republic | Tschechien (B), Oldřich Liska, Václav
Flegl, 1922–23

Commerical School | Handelsschule, Cintorínska Ulica 1479/4, Nitra |
Neutra, Slovakia | Slowakei (B), Klement Šilinger, 1922–26

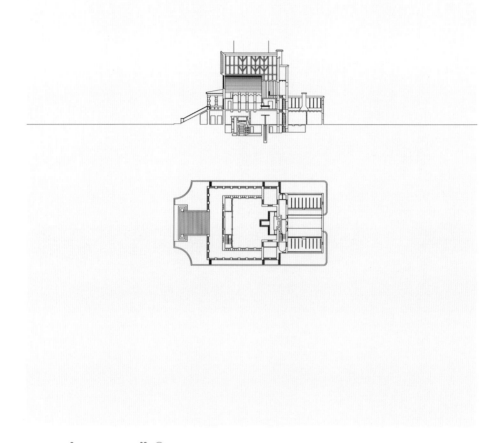

0   20

37
Crematorium | Krematorium, Pod Břízkami 990, Pardubice | Pardu-
bitz, Czech Republic | Tschechien (B), Pavel Janák, 1921–23

38

Coking Coal Tower, Szczecin Gas Plant | Kokskohlenturm Stettiner
Gaswerke, Koksowa 5, Szczecin | Stettin, Poland | Polen (A), Adolf
Thesmacher, 1925–26

39

School of Architecture, Academy of Fine Arts | Architekturschule Akademie der Bildenden Künste, U akademie 172/2, Prague | Prag | Praha, Czech Republic | Tschechien (J), Josef Gočár, Jan Kotěra, 1919–24

40

Hussite Church | Hussitenkirche, Koněvova 665, Turnov | Turnau,
Czech Republic | Tschechien (B), Vladimír Krýš, 1937–39

41

Municipal Theatre | Stadttheater, Henryka Sienkiewicza 3, Chorzów |
Königshütte, Poland | Polen (I), 1940?

42
Chapel, Osobowice Cemetery | Kapelle Friedhof Oswitz, Oso-
bowicka 59, Wrocław | Breslau, Poland | Polen (D), Max Berg,
Albert Kempter, 1920–21

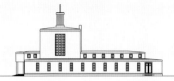

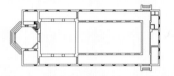

0　　　　　　20

43
Bethlehem Chapel | Bethlehem-Kapelle, Prokopova 216/4, Prague |
Prag | Praha, Czech Republic | Tschechien (J), Emil Králíček, 1912–13

44

Hussite Church | Hussitenkirche, Nádražní 389, Semily | Semil,
Czech Republic | Tschechien (B), Vladimír Krýš, 1938

45
Municipal Cinema and Theatre (Municipal Theatre) | Lichtspiel und
Stadttheater (Stadttheater), Mikulášská 911/21, Krnov | Jägerndorf,
Czech Republic | Tschechien (B), Leo Kammel, 1927–28

46
Domovina Housing Cooperative Workers' Flats | Beamten- und Arbeiter-
wohnkolonie der Baugenossenschaft Domovina, U Domoviny 1, Jarošova
16–26, Znojmo | Znaim, Czech Republic | Tschechien (B), Otakar
Novotny, 1920–26

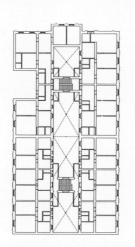

0   20

47

Flats and Shops | Wohn- und Geschäftshaus, U Nádraží 1294, Turnov |
Turnau, Czech Republic | Tschechien (B), 1922–24

48

Gärtner Building | Haus Gärtner, Sokolovské náměstí 277, Liberec |
Reichenberg, Czech Republic | Tschechien (B), Ferdinand Elstner,
1929

49

Dam and Hydroelectric Station | Stau- und Wasserkraftwerk,
Poděbrady 71, Poděbrady | Podiebrad, Czech Republic |
Tschechien (B), Božimír Kozák, 1923

50

Hansa Building | Hansa-Haus, Stanisława Webera 4, Bytom |
Beuthen, Poland | Polen (H), Felix Wieczorek, 1925

51
Diamond Building | Geschäftshaus Diamant, Spálená 82/4, Prague |
Prag | Praha, Czech Republic | Tschechien (J), Matěj Blecha, Emil
Králíček, 1912–13

52

Aedicula Framing for St Nepomuk Statue | Ädikula für Statue des
Heiligen Nepomuk, Spálená 82/4, Prague | Prag | Praha, Czech
Republic | Tschechien (J), Matěj Blecha, Emil Králíček, 1912–13

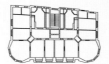

51, 52

Diamond Building with Aedicula Framing for St Nepomuk Statue |
Geschäftshaus Diamant mit Ädikula für Statue des Heiligen Nepomuk,
Spálená 82/4, Prague | Prag | Praha, Czech Republic | Tschechien (J),
Matěj Blecha, Emil Králíček, 1912–13

0   20

53
Sanatorium | Kurhaus, Masarykovo náměstí 6, Lázně Bohdaneč |
Bochdanetsch, Czech Republic | Tschechien (B), Josef Gočár, 1912–13

Sanatorium | Kurhaus, Masarykovo náměstí 6, Lázně Bohdaneč |
Bochdanetsch, Czech Republic | Tschechien (B), Josef Gočár, 1912–13

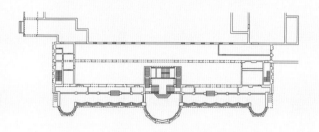

0   20

Gates, Ďáblice Cemetery | Portalanlage Friedhof Ďáblice, Ďáblický,
Prague | Prag | Praha, Czech Republic | Tschechien (J), Vlastislav
Hofman, 1912–13?

55

Flats | Wohnhäuser, Opawska 72–76, Ludwika Waryńskiego 17–19,
23–25, 22–26, Racibórz | Ratibor, Poland | Polen (B), 1926–30

56

Anna Tille Flats and Shops | Wohn- und Geschäftshaus Anna Tille,
Na Skřivance 150/1, Děčín | Tetschen, Czech Republic | Tschechien
(B), Josef Hiecke, Emil Hiecke, 1929

57
Protestant Church | Evangelische Kirche, Myslenická 134/3195,
Grinava | Grünau, Slovakia | Slowakei (B), Hans Jaksch, Siegfried
Theiss, ca. 1931

58
St Mary's Secondary School | Marien-Lyzeum, Królowej Bony 13,
Gliwice | Gleiwitz, Poland | Polen (G), 1927–29

59
Zeipau Water Tower | Wasserturm Zeipau, Szczepanów, Jankowa
Żagańska | Hansdorf, Poland | Polen (A), Otto Bartning, 1922

Water Tower | Wasserturm, Kolejowa, Zbąszynek | Neu Bentschen,
Poland | Polen (A), Bruno Möhring, ca. 1923

61

Scrubbing Tower, Paper Mill | Rieselerturm Papierfabrik,
Franciszkańska 26, Koszalin | Köslin, Poland | Polen (A), Oskar
Kaufmann, 1919–20

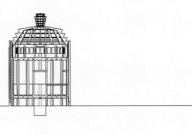

0   20

Crematorium | Krematorium, Jihlavská 756/1, Brno | Brünn, Czech
Republic | Tschechien (B), Ernst [Arnošt] Wiesner, 1925–30

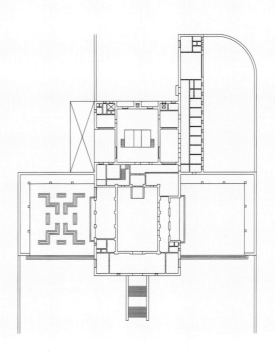

0   20

63
Club House, Szczecin Yachting Club | Vereinshaus Stettiner Jacht-
klub, Lipowa 5, Szczecin | Stettin, Poland | Polen (A), Gustav Gauss,
1924

Flats | Wohnhaus, Legnicka 64, Wrocław | Breslau, Poland | Polen (D)

65

Flats (Police Headquarters) | Wohnhaus (Polizeipräsidium), Adama
Asnyka 3, Legnica | Liegnitz, Poland | Polen (C), 1928–29

66

Salem Monastery Secondary School (State Office of Repatriation,
School for Handicapped Children) | Lyzeum für Stift Salem (Staatliches
Repatriierungsamt, Sonderpädagogisches Zentrum), Jagiellońska 65,
Szczecin | Stettin (A), Poland | Polen

Girls' Elementary School (Secondary School No. 1) | Mädchen-Volks-
schule (Gymnasium Nr. 1), Kościuszki 7, Kostrzyn nad Odrą | Küstrin,
Poland | Polen (A), Walter Ernst Hecht, 1929–30

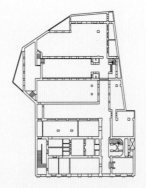

68

Štenc Building | Haus Štenc, Salvátorská 931/8, Prague | Prag | Praha,
Czech Republic | Tschechien (J), Otakar Novotny, 1909–10

69
Laichter Building | Haus Laichter, Chopinova 1543/4, Prague | Prag |
Praha, Czech Republic | Tschechien (J), Jan Kotěra, 1908–09

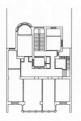

0   20

70

Urbánek Buidling (Mozarteum) | Haus Urbánek (Mozarteum),
Jungmannova 748/30, Prague | Prag | Praha, Czech Republic |
Tschechien (J), Jan Kotěra, 1911–13

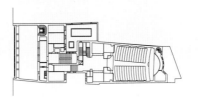

0   20

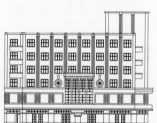

○＿＿＿＿＿＿＿20

71

Insurance Company Riunione Adriatica di Sicurtá Flats and Shops
(Grand Flats and Shops) | Wohn- und Geschäftshaus Versicherung
Riunione Adriatica di Sicurtá (Wohn- und Geschäftshaus Grand),
Velká Hradební 2, Ústí nad Labem | Aussig, Czech Republic |
Tschechien (B), Fritz Lehmann, 1928–29

72

Police Prison | Polizeigefängnis, Daszyńskiego 18, Legnica | Liegnitz,
Poland | Polen (C), Paul Oehlmann, 1929–30

73

Extension, Catholic School (Primary School) | Erweiterung Katholische
Schule (Grundschule), Rycerska 13, Legnica | Liegnitz, Poland | Polen (C),
Paul Oehlmann, 1929–30

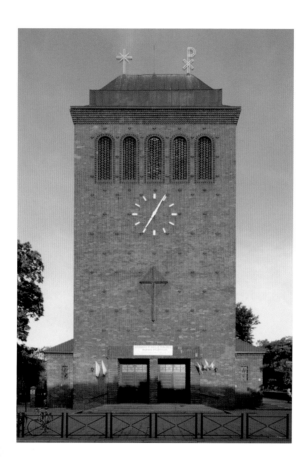

74

Church of the Holy Family | Kirche Heilige Familie, Monte Cassino 68,
Wrocław | Breslau, Poland | Polen (D), Kurt Langer, 1928–30

75

Girls' House, Home for the Blind (Primary School No. 47) | Mäd-
chenhaus der Blindenanstalt (Grundschule Nr. 47), Jagiellońska 59,
Szczecin | Stettin, Poland | Polen (A), 1928

Heimat Flats | Wohnhäuser Heimat, Działkowa 12–20, Legnica |
Liegnitz, Poland | Polen (C), Konrad Beicht, 1927–28

Kostrzyn Guesthouse | Küstriner Hof, Piastowska 8, Kostrzyn nad
Odrą | Küstrin (A), Poland | Polen

78

Public Health Insurance Company | Allgemeine Ortskrankenkasse,
Senatorska 1, Legnica | Liegnitz, Poland | Polen (C), Konrad Beicht,
ca. 1927

79
Tanners' School (Vocational School for Mechanical Engineering) |
Gerberschule (Fachschule für Maschinenbau), Hradecká 1a/647,
Hradec Králové | Königgrätz, Czech Republic | Tschechien (K),
Josef Gočár, 1923–24

Epilepsy Hospital | Epilepsiekrankenhaus, Stabłowicka 147–149,
Wrocław | Breslau, Poland | Polen (D), Max Berg, Georg Müller,
1912–13

81

Municipal Museum (East Bohemian Museum) | Stadtmuseum
(Ostböhmisches Museum), Eliščino nábřeží 465/7, Hradec Králové |
Königgrätz, Czech Republic | Tschechien (K), Jan Kotěra, 1909–13

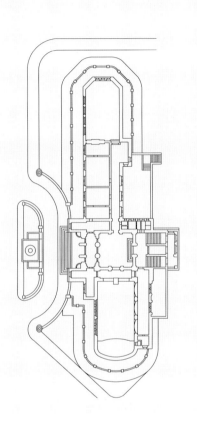

0   20

82

Rašín Secondary School (Josef Kajetán Tyl Secondary School) |
Rašín-Gymnasium (Josef Kajetán Tyl-Gymnasium), Tylovo nábřeží
12/682, Hradec Králové | Königgrätz, Czech Republic | Tschechien
(K), Josef Gočár, 1923–27

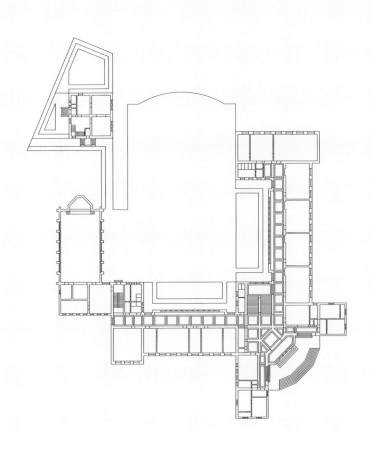

O   20

83

Extension, Secondary School | Erweiterung Oberlyzeum, Tadeusza
Kościuszki, Władysława Reymonta, Opole | Oppeln, Poland |
Polen (B), after | nach 1924

84

Secondary School (Faculty of Electrical Engineering, Silesian Technical University) | Gymnasium (Elektrotechnische Fakultät Schlesische Technische Hochschule), Bolesława Krzywoustego, Akademicka, Gliwice | Gleiwitz, Poland | Polen (G), Gustav Kassbaum, Arno Kluge, 1926–28 [Additions until | Ergänzungen bis 1932]

85

Church of the Lord's Most Sacred Heart | Kirche des heiligsten Herzens
des Herrn, Horní náměstí 12, Jablonec nad Nisou | Gablonz an der
Neiße, Czech Republic | Tschechien (B), Josef Zasche, 1930–32

Polchow Groundwater Works | Grundwasserwerk Polchow,
Wodociągowa 5, Szczecin | Stettin, Poland | Polen (A)

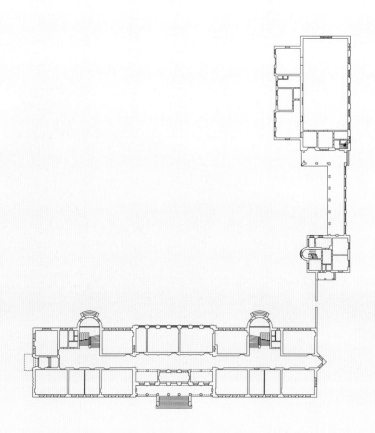

87
Pestalozzi School | Pestalozzischule, Jedności Robotniczej 10, Głogów |
Glogau, Poland | Polen (A), Erwin Griesinger, 1926–28

88
Flats and Shops (PKO Bank Polski) | Wohn- und Geschäftshaus
(PKO Bank Polski), Plac Piastów, Bohaterów Getta Warszawskiego 2,
Gliwice | Gleiwitz, Poland | Polen (G)

89

Flats and Shops | Wohn- und Geschäftshaus, Plac Inwalidów 6,
Królewska 1, Pomorska 1, Henryka Sienkiewicza 2, Kraków | Krakau,
Poland | Polen (B), W. Nowakowski, ca. 1929

90

Station | Bahnhof, Dworcowa, Legnica | Liegnitz, Poland | Polen (C),
1922–29

91

Hotel Admiral Palast | Hotel Admiralspalast, Wolności 305, Zabrze |
Hindenburg O.S., Poland | Polen (F), Richard Bielenberg, Josef Moser,
1924–28

92

New Synagogue | Neue Synagoge, Jozefa Miloslava Hurbana 220/11,
Žilina | Sillein, Slovakia | Slowakei (B), Peter Behrens, 1929–31

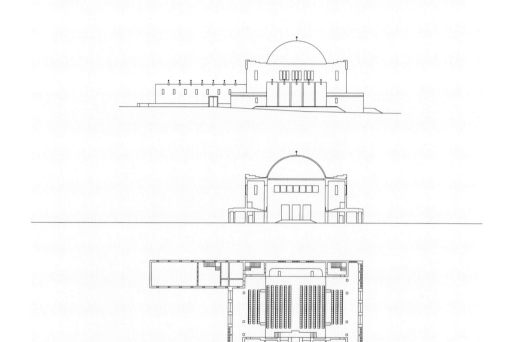

93
St Michael the Archangel | St. Michael, Fabryczna 19, Lublin,
Poland | Polen (A), Oskar Sosnowski, 1930?–38?

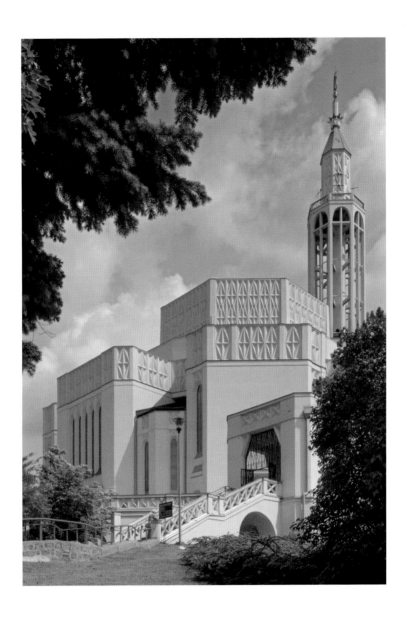

94
Church of Saint Roch | St. Rochus, Księdza Adama Abramowicza 1,
Białystok, Poland | Polen (A), Oskar Sosnowski, 1927–44

94

Church of St Roch | St. Rochus, Księdza Adama Abramowicza 1,
Białystok, Poland | Polen (A), Oskar Sosnowski, 1927–44

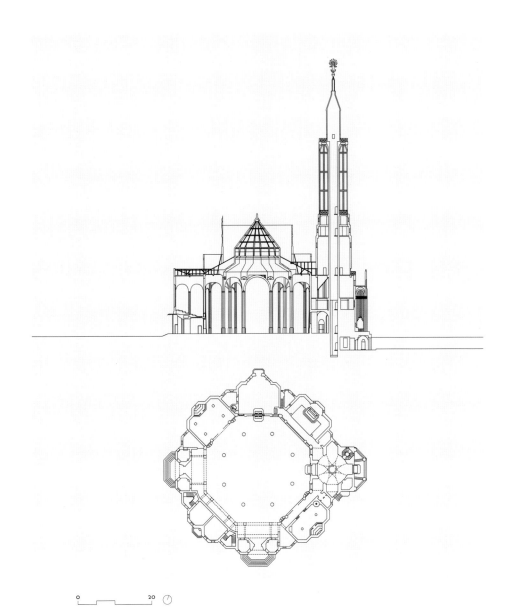

95
Offices Karlsruhe Insurance Company | Verwaltungsgebäude Karls-
ruher Lebensversicherung, Michała Bałuckiego 2, Wrocław | Breslau,
Poland | Polen (D), Moritz Hadda, Wilhelm Schlesinger, 1922

96

Flats | Wohnhaus, Neklanova 56/2, Prague | Prag | Praha, Czech
Republic | Tschechien (J), Antonín Belada, Josef Chochol, 1911–13

97
Hodeck Building | Haus Hodeck, Neklanova 98/30, Prague | Prag |
Praha, Czech Republic | Tschechien (J), Josef Chochol, 1913–14

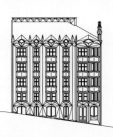

0   20

Boarding School | Internatsgebäude, 29. augusta 10, Bratislava |
Pressburg, Slovakia | Slowakei (L), František Krupka, 1925

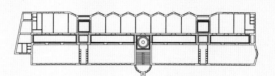

O [____] 20 🕐

99

Flats | Wohnhäuser, Bubeníkova 526, Čechovo nábřeží 527, 528,
Polská 529, 530, Pardubice | Pardubitz, Czech Republic |
Tschechien (B), Oldřich Liska?, 1920–24

Institute of Sociology, Slovak Academy of Science | Institut für
Sozialwissenschaften Slowakische Akademie der Wissenschaften,
Klemensova 2522/19, Bratislava | Pressburg, Slovakia | Slowakei (L),
1921

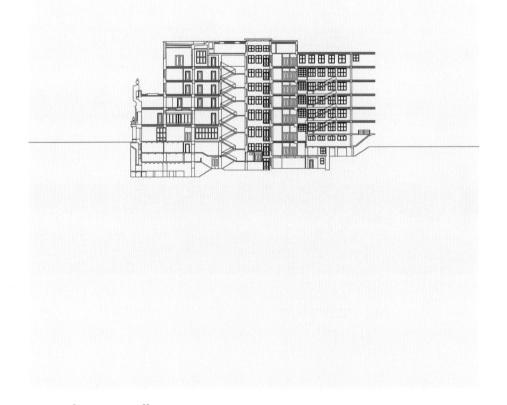

101

Conversion, Anglo Bank | Umbau Anglobank, Hybernská 1034/5,
Prague | Prag | Praha, Czech Republic | Tschechien (J), Josef Gočár,
1923–26

102
Junkerstrasse Offices | Geschäftshaus Junkerstraße, Ofiar
Oświęcimskich 38–40, Wrocław | Breslau, Poland | Polen (D),
Hans Poelzig, 1911–13

Junkerstrasse Offices | Geschäftshaus Junkerstraße, Ofiar
Oświęcimskich 38–40, Wrocław | Breslau, Poland | Polen (D),
Hans Poelzig, 1911–13

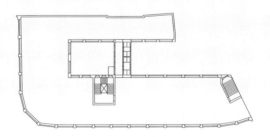

0   20

103
Municipal Savings Bank | Stadtsparkasse, Fosa Staromiejska 1a,
Toruń | Thorn, Poland | Polen (A), Jerzy Wierzbicki, 1935–36

Extension, Anglo-Czechoslovakian Bank | Erweiterung Anglo-Tschechoslowakische Bank, Masarykovo náměstí 5/510, 6/511, 8/628, Hradec Králové | Königgrätz, Czech Republic | Tschechien (K), Josef Gočár, Josef Fňouk, 1923–25

105
Offices and Factory, Associated Workshops | Büro- und Fabrikgebäude
Vereinigte Werkstätten, Sušilova 247/15, Třebíč | Trebitsch, Czech
Republic | Tschechien (B), Josef Gočár, 1919–22

Anglo-Czechoslovakian Bank | Anglo-Tschechoslowakische Bank,
Čelakovského 2/642, Hradec Králové | Königgrätz, Czech Republic |
Tschechien (K), Josef Gočár, 1922–23

107
Radio Station (Golf Club) | Radiostation (Golfklub), Na Zálesí 530,
Poděbrady | Podiebrad, Czech Republic | Tschechien (B), Antonín
Engel, 1914–23

108

Flats and Shops | Wohn- und Geschäftshaus, Na Hradbách 93,
Kolín | Kolin, Czech Republic | Tschechien (B), Jaroslav Böhm,
Jindřich Freiwald, 1921–23

Flats and Shops | Wohn- und Geschäftshaus, Jungmannovo náměstí
764/4, 28. října 764/8, Prague | Prag | Praha, Czech Republic |
Tschechien (J), Rudolf Stockar, 1920–22

110

House of the Black Madonna | Haus zur Schwarzen Muttergottes,
Ovocny trh 569/19, Prague | Prag | Praha, Czech Republic |
Tschechien (J), Josef Gočár, 1911–12

House of the Black Madonna | Haus zur Schwarzen Muttergottes,
Ovocny trh 569/19, Prague | Prag | Praha, Czech Republic |
Tschechien (J), Josef Gočár, 1911–12

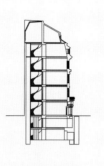

0   20

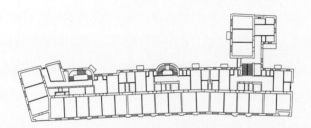

111
Flats | Wohnhäuser, Štetinová 1–5, Bratislava | Pressburg, Slovakia |
Slowakei (L), Klement Šilinger, 1921–22

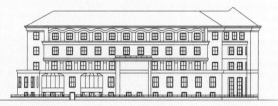

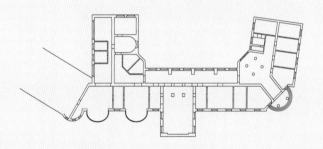

Institute of Anatomy, Comenius University | Anatomisches Institut
Comenius-Universität, Sasinkova 2626/2, Bratislava | Pressburg,
Slovakia | Slowakei (L), Klement Šilinger, 1924?–27?

Flats | Wohnhäuser, Resslova 601/33, 602/31, 603/29, Hradec
Králové | Königgrätz, Czech Republic | Tschechien (K)

114

Flats | Wohnhaus, Resslova 600/35, Hradec Králové | Königgrätz,
Czech Republic | Tschechien (K)

115
Flats | Wohnhaus, Ruská 866/20, 930/22, Děčín | Tetschen, Czech
Republic | Tschechien (B), Jaroslav Herink, 1923

Flats | Wohnhaus, Heydukova 2148/23, Bratislava | Pressburg,
Slovakia | Slowakei (L), Klement Šilinger, 1923

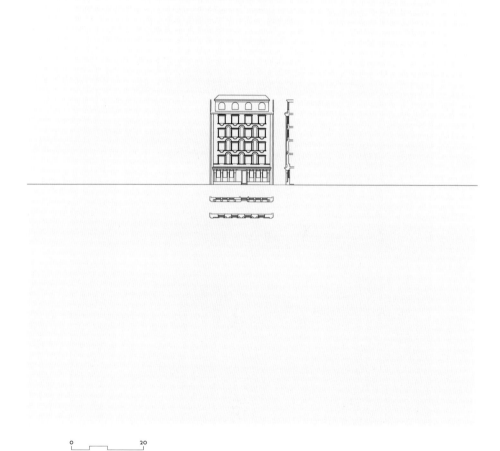

0   20

117

Teachers' Cooperative Flats | Wohnhaus der Lehrergenossenschaft,
Kamenická 811/35, Prague | Prag | Praha, Czech Republic |
Tschechien (J), Otakar Novotny, 1923–24

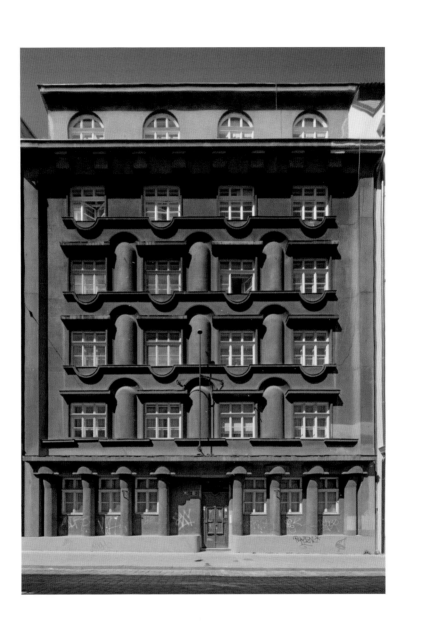

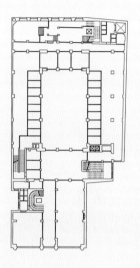

0   20

118

Legio Bank | Bank der tschechoslowakischen Legionen, Na poříčí
1046/24, Prague | Prag | Praha, Czech Republic | Tschechien (J), Josef
Gočár, Otto Gutfreund, 1921–23

119

Insurance Company Riunione Adriatica di Sicurtá Offices and Shops
(Adria Palace) | Büro- und Geschäftsgebäude Versicherung Riunione
Adriatica di Sicurtá (Adria-Palast), Jungmannova 36/31, Prague |
Prag | Praha, Czech Republic | Tschechien (J), Pavel Janák, Josef
Zasche, 1922–25

Offices, Škoda Factory | Verwaltungsgebäude Škoda-Werke, Jung-
mannova 35/29, Prague | Prag | Praha, Czech Republic | Tschechien
(J), Pavel Janák, 1923–26

Police Headquarters | Polizeipräsidium, Špitálska 2211/14, Bratislava |
Pressburg, Slovakia | Slowakei (L), František Krupka, 1922

Faculty of Law, Charles University | Juristische Fakultät Karls-
Universität, Náměstí Curieových 901/7, Prague | Prag | Praha,
Czech Republic | Tschechien (J), Jan Kotěra, 1926–31

123
Head Offices of State Railways | Hauptverwaltung der Staatseisen-
bahn, Klemensova 2526/8, Bratislava | Pressburg, Slovakia | Slowakei
(L), Alois Balán, Jiří Grossmann, 1925–27

Communal Flats | Gemeindewohnhäuser, Tovární 1264/6, 1265/8,
1270/10, Prague | Prag | Praha, Czech Republic | Tschechien (J),
Rudolf Hrabě, 1921–23

125

Teachers' Cooperative Flats | Wohnhäuser der Lehrergenossen-
schaft, Elišky Krásnohorské 123/10-14, Prague | Prag | Praha,
Czech Republic | Tschechien (J), Otakar Novotny, 1919–21

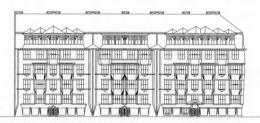

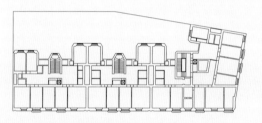

 0   20

125

Teachers' Cooperative Flats | Wohnhäuser der Lehrergenossen-
schaft, Elišky Krásnohorské 123/10-14, Prague | Prag | Praha,
Czech Republic | Tschechien (J), Otakar Novotny, 1919–21

Main Building, School of Economics | Hauptgebäude Höhere
Handelsschule (Wirtschaftshochschule), Aleja Niepodległości 162,
Warsaw | Warschau | Warszawa, Poland | Polen (E), Jan Witkiewicz
[Koszczyc], 1950–53 (Design | Entwurf 1924)

127
Annex, School of Economics | Nebengebäude Höhere Handelsschule
(Wirtschaftshochschule), Rakowiecka 24, Warsaw | Warschau |
Warszawa, Poland | Polen (E), Jan Witkiewicz [Koszczyc], 1925?–26?

128

Library, School of Economics | Bibliothek Höhere Handelsschule
(Wirtschaftshochschule), Rakowiecka 22, Warsaw | Warschau |
Warszawa, Poland | Polen (E), Jan Witkiewicz [Koszczyc], 1928?–31?

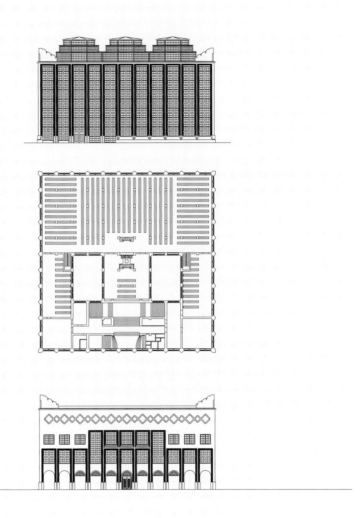

0   20

129

Breda & Weinstein Department Store | Kaufhaus Breda & Weinstein,
Náměstí Republiky 160/11, Opava | Troppau, Czech Republic |
Tschechien (B), Leopold Bauer, Julius Lundwall, 1927–28

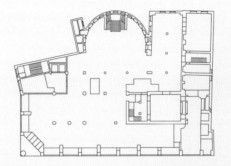

129
Breda & Weinstein Department Store | Kaufhaus Breda & Weinstein,
Náměstí Republiky 160/11, Opava | Troppau, Czech Republic |
Tschechien (B), Leopold Bauer, Julius Lundwall, 1927–28

Public Health Insurance Company | Allgemeine Ortskranken-
kasse, Wałowej 27, Gdańsk | Danzig, Poland | Polen (A), Adolf
Bielefeldt, 1925–27

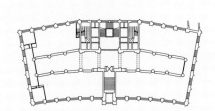

0   20

131
Winternitz Factory | Fabrikgebäude Winternitz, Mezi Mosty, Pardubice |
Pardubitz, Czech Republic | Tschechien (B), Josef Gočár, 1910–19

132

St Anthony | St. Antonius, Mikołaja Kopernika 1, Chorzów | Königs-
hütte, Poland | Polen (I), Adam Ballenstedt, 1930–34

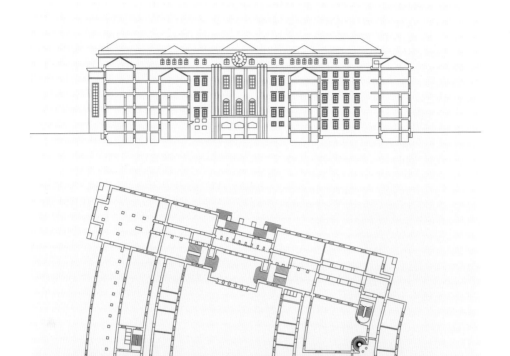

133

Police Headquarters | Polizeipräsidium, Podwale 31–33, Wrocław |
Breslau, Poland | Polen (D), Rudolf Fernholz, 1925–27

Police Headquarters | Polizeipräsidium, Podwale 31–33, Wrocław |
Breslau, Poland | Polen (D), Rudolf Fernholz, 1925–27

Spolchemie Offices | Verwaltungsgebäude Spolchemie, Revoluční
1930/86, Ústí nad Labem | Aussig, Czech Republic | Tschechien (B),
Hans Max Kühne, 1929–30

135
Postal Cheque Office (Post and Telecommunication Museum) | Post-scheckamt (Museum für Post- und Fernmeldewesen), Zygmunta Krasińskiego 1–9, Wrocław | Breslau, Poland | Polen (D), Lothar Neumann, 1926–29

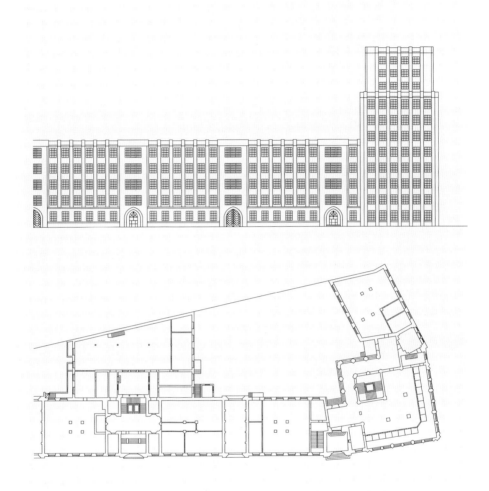

O   20

Centennial Hall | Jahrhunderthalle, Zygmunta Wróblewskiego 1,
Wrocław | Breslau, Poland | Polen (D), Max Berg, 1911–13

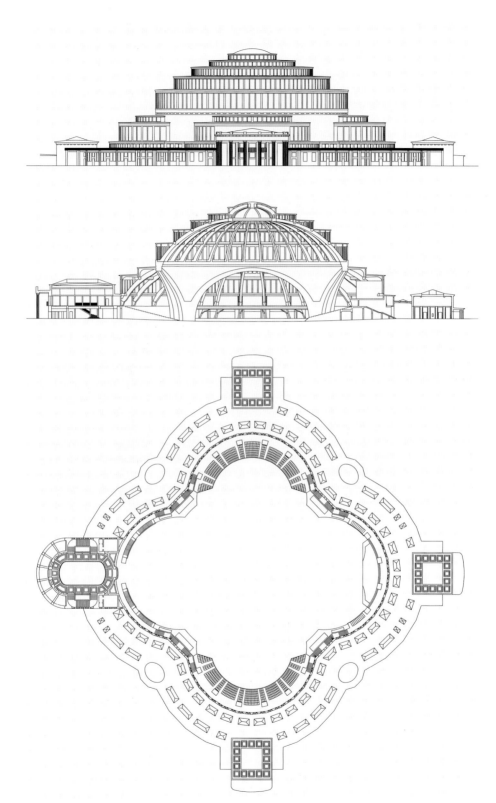

0   20

Centennial Hall | Jahrhunderthalle, Zygmunta Wróblewskiego 1,
Wrocław | Breslau, Poland | Polen (D), Max Berg, 1911–13

137

Anna Mine | Annagrube, Księdza Pawła Skwary 25, Pszów | Pschow, Poland | Polen (B), Hans Poelzig, 1913–15

138

Church of the Immaculate Conception | Kirche Unbefleckte Empfängnis Mariä, Długa 29, Zbąszynek | Neu Bentschen, Poland | Polen (A), Wilhelm Beringer?, 1929–30

139

Northern Hydroelectric Station | Wasserkraftwerk Nord, most Pomorski, Wrocław | Breslau, Poland | Polen (D), Wilhelm Anders, Max Berg, Paul Schreiber [sometimes | manchmal: Schneider], 1924–25

140

Decastello Building | Haus Decastello, Karmelitská 268/26, Prague | Prag | Praha, Czech Republic | Tschechien (J), Emil Králíček, 1911–13

141

District Health Insurance Company | Bezirkskrankenkasse, Nerudova 321/11, Zahradníkova 321/6, Brno | Brünn, Czech Republic | Tschechien (B), Jindřich Kumpošt, 1922–24

142

Eichendorff Secondary School | Eichendorff-Gymnasium (Fakultät für Energie- und Umwelttechnik Schlesische Technische Hochschule), Stanisława Konarskiego 22, Gliwice | Gleiwitz, Poland | Polen (G), Karl Schabik, 1928–30

143

Fatherland House | Haus Vaterland, 11 Listopada 40, Piła | Schneidemühl, Poland | Polen (A)

144

First President Dr. Proske School (A. Mickiewicz Secondary School) | Oberpräsident-Dr.-Proske-Schule (A. Mickiewicz-Gymnasium), Kardynała Stefana Wyszyńskiego 3, Racibórz | Ratibor, Poland | Polen (B), Klemens [Clemenz] Raffelsiefen, 1926–28

145

Flats | Wohnhaus, Heřmanova 1168/24, Prague | Prag | Praha, Czech Republic | Tschechien (J), Václav Zákostelka, 1913

146

Flats | Wohnhaus, Ignacego Chrzanowskiego 1b, Bytom | Beuthen, Poland | Polen (H), 1926

147

Flats | Wohnhaus, Legionárska 1, Bratislava | Pressburg, Slovakia | Slowakei (L)

148

Flats | Wohnhäuser, 29. augusta 38, Karadžičova 3, Bratislava | Pressburg, Slovakia | Slowakei (L), Klement Šilinger

149

Flats | Wohnhaus, 29. augusta 28–34, Bratislava | Pressburg, Slovakia | Slowakei (L)

150

Flats | Wohnhäuser, Legionárska 3–7, Bratislava | Pressburg, Slovakia | Slowakei (L)

151

Flats and Shops | Wohn- und Geschäftshauser, Plac Dworcowy, Zbąszynek | Neu Bentschen, Poland | Polen (A), Wilhelm Beringer?

152

Flats and Shops | Wohn- und Geschäftshaus, Pražská 99, Kolín | Kolin, Czech Republic | Tschechien (B), J. V. Petřík

153

House at the Stone Table | Haus zum steinernen Tisch, Ječná 550/1, Prague | Prag | Praha, Czech Republic | Tschechien (J), Theodor Petřík, 1911–12

154

House of the Jagiellonian University Professors | Haus der Professoren der Jagiellonen-Universität, Plac Inwalidów 4, Kraków | Krakau, Poland | Polen (B), Piotr Jurkiewicz, Ludwik Wojtycko, Stefan Żeleński, ca. 1929

155

Institute of Aerodynamics, Warsaw University of Technology (Museum, Warsaw University of Technology) | Institut für Aerodynamik Technische Universität Warschau (Museum Technische Universität Warschau), Nowowiejska 24, Warsaw | Warschau | Warszawa, Poland | Polen (E), Franciszek Lilpop, 1930s | 1930er

156

Offices and Flats, Public Pension Insurance Company | Büro- und Wohngebäude Allgemeine Pensionsversicherung, Kounicova 294/63, Nerudova 294/14, Brno | Brünn, Czech Republic | Tschechien (B), Jindřich Kumpošt, 1921–22

157

Offices? | Bürogebäude?, Pocztowa 1, Piła | Schneidemühl, Poland | Polen (A)

158

Police Station (Faculty of Dentistry, Silesian Medical University) | Polizeiamt (Zahnmedizinische Fakultät Schlesische Medizinische Universität), Plac Akademicki 17, Bytom | Beuthen, Poland | Polen (H), Wilhelm Bahlsen, 1925

159

Private Civil Servants' Health Insurance Company | Krankenkasse der Privatbeamten und -bediensteten, Kounicova 299/42, Zahradníkova 299/10, Brno | Brünn, Czech Republic | Tschechien (B), Jaroslav Syřiště, 1923

160

Shops | Geschäftshaus, Plac Rynek 11, Żary | Sorau, Poland | Polen (A)

161

St Joseph | St. Joseph, Franklina Roosevelta 104, Zabrze | Hindenburg O.S., Poland | Polen (F), Dominikus Böhm, 1929–31

162

St Joseph the Husband | St. Josef der Bräutigam, Czerniakowska 137, Warsaw | Warschau | Warszawa, Poland | Polen (E), Karol Jankowski, Franciszek Lilpop, 1922–26

163

Švanda Theatre | Švanda-Theater, Štefánikova 6/57, Prague | Prag | Praha, Czech Republic | Tschechien (J), Ladislav Machoň, 1918–20

MAPS
INDEX OF BUILDINGS
ARCHITECTS

KARTEN
GEBÄUDEREGISTER
ARCHITEKTEN

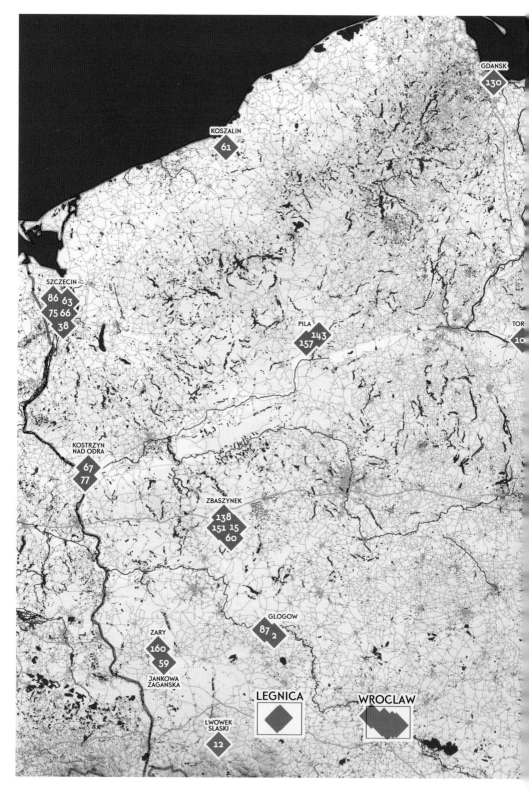

GDANSK 130

KOSZALIN 61

SZCZECIN 86 63 75 66 38

PILA 143 157

TOR 10

KOSTRZYN NAD ODRA 67 77

ZBASZYNEK 138 151 15 60

GLOGOW 87 2

ZARY 160 59

JANKOWA ZAGANSKA

LEGNICA

WROCLAW

LWOWEK SLASKI 12

A   2, 6, 12, 15, 38, 59, 60, 61, 63, 66, 67, 75, 77, 86, 87, 93, 94, 103, 130, 138, 143, 151, 157, 160

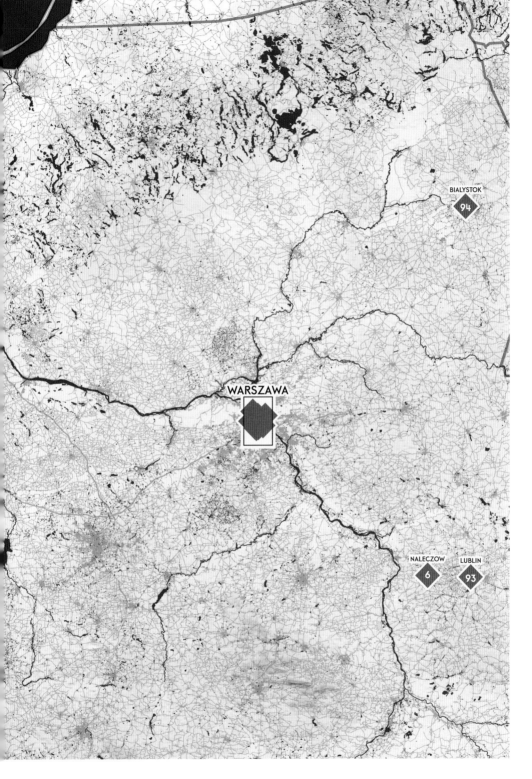

WARSZAWA

BIALYSTOK
94

NALECZOW
6

LUBLIN
93

0   50   100

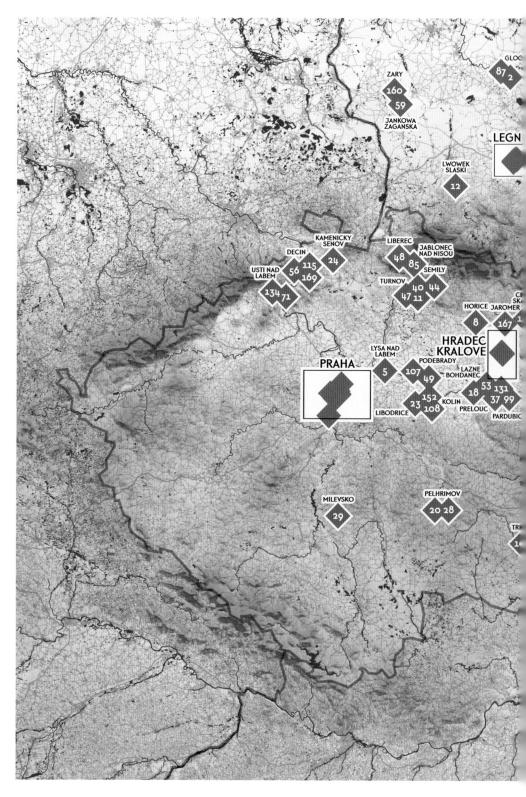

B   2, 5, 7, 8, 10, 11, 12, 14, 18, 20, 21, 22, 23, 24, 28, 29, 32, 33, 34, 35, 36, 37, 40, 44, 45, 46, 47, 48, 49, 53, 55, 56, 57, 59, 62, 71, 83, 85, 87, 89, 92, 99, 105, 107, 108, 115, 129, 131, 134, 137, 141, 144, 152, 154, 156, 159, 160, 164, 165, 166, 167, 169

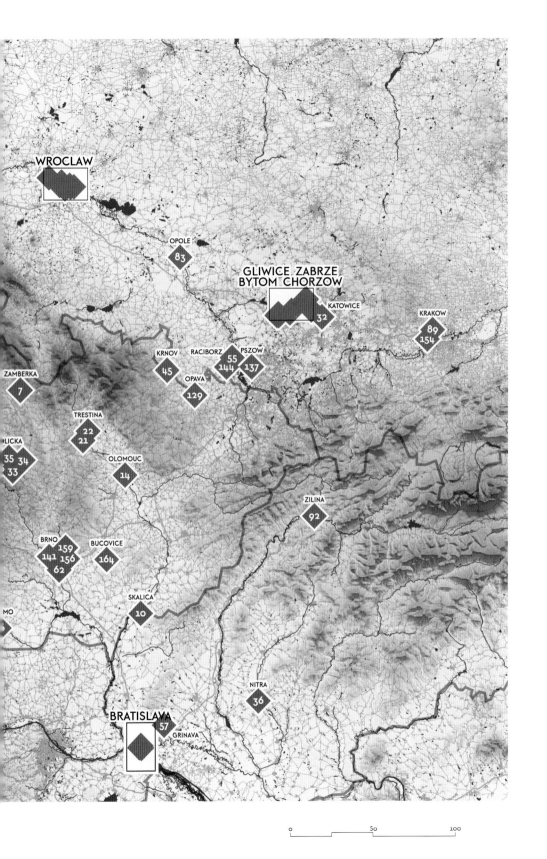

WROCLAW

OPOLE
83

GLIWICE ZABRZE
BYTOM CHORZOW
KATOWICE
32

KRAKOW
89
154

ZAMBERKA
7

KRNOV
45

RACIBORZ
PSZOW
55
144
137

OPAVA
129

TRESTINA
22
21

OLICKA
35 34
33

OLOMOUC
14

ZILINA
92

BRNO
159
141 156
62

BUCOVICE
164

SKALICA
10

MO

NITRA
36

BRATISLAVA
57
GRINAVA

0   50   100

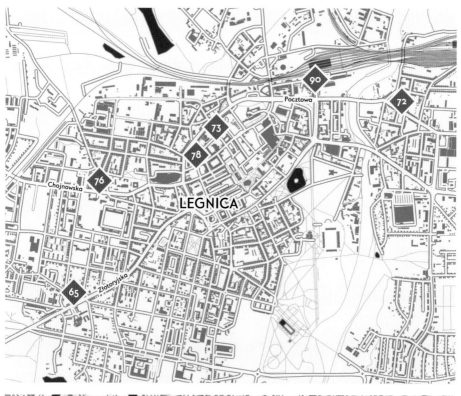

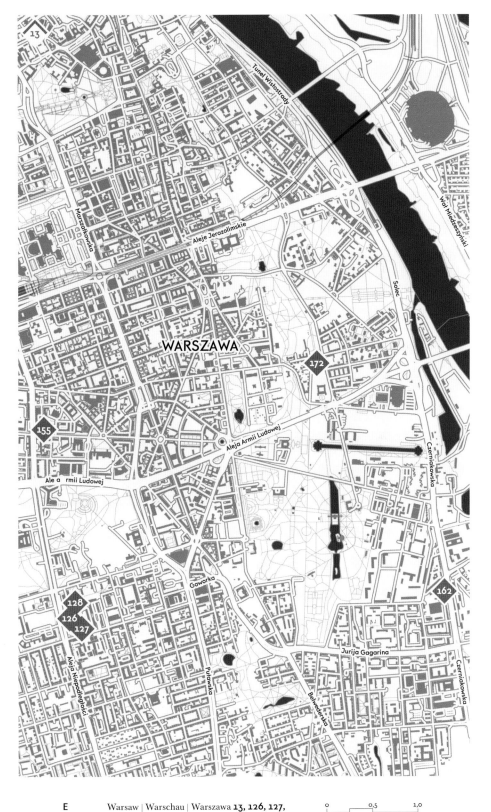

E   Warsaw | Warschau | Warszawa **13, 126, 127,
           128, 155, 162, 172**

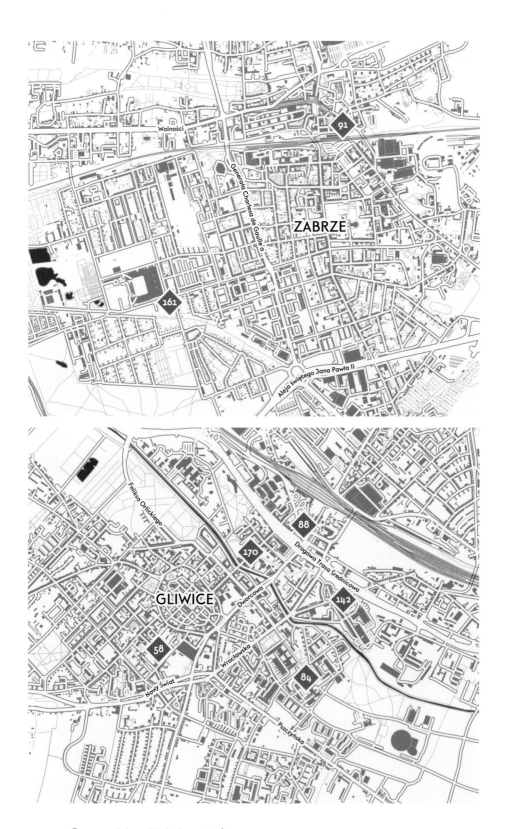

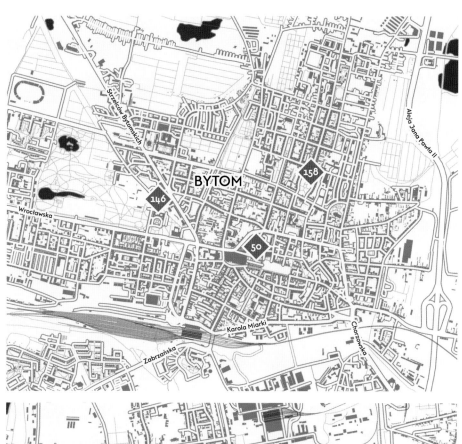

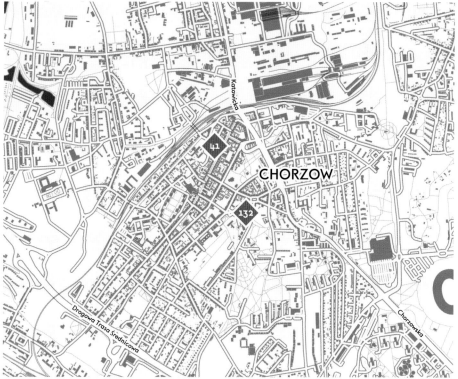

H   Bytom | Beuthen **50, 146, 158**
I   Chorzów | Königshütte **41, 132**

0   0,5   1,0

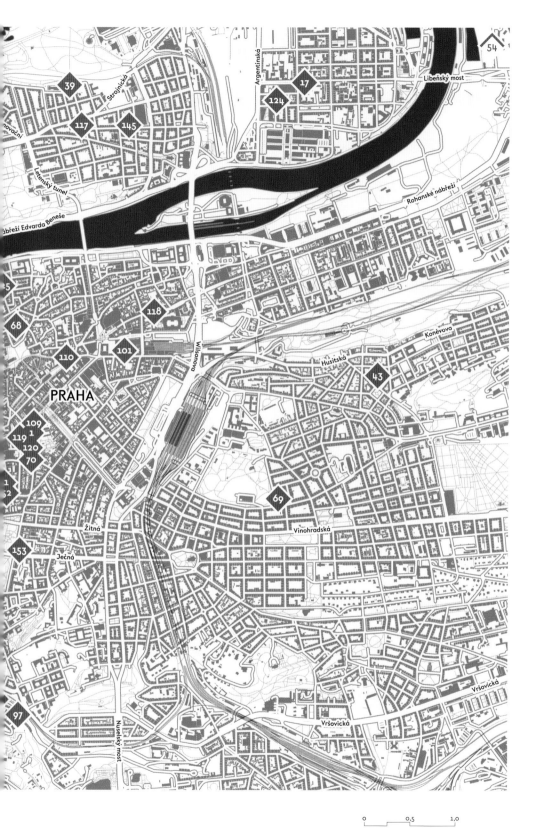

PRAHA

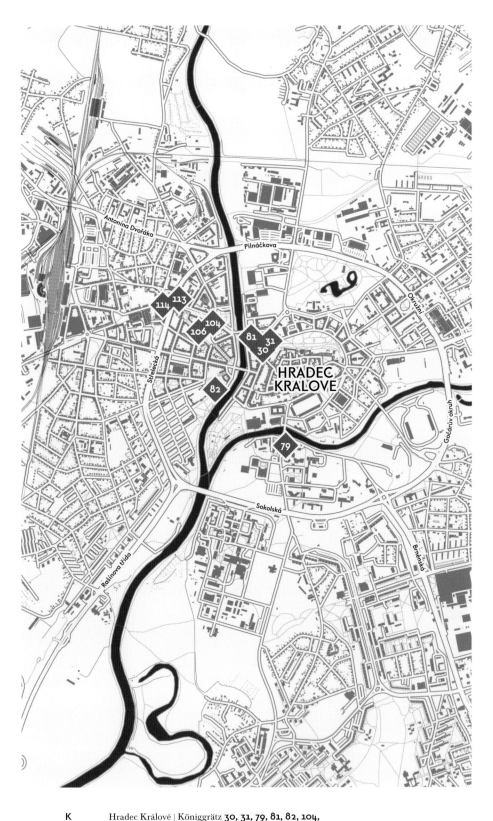

K   Hradec Králové | Königgrätz 30, 31, 79, 81, 82, 104, 106, 113, 114

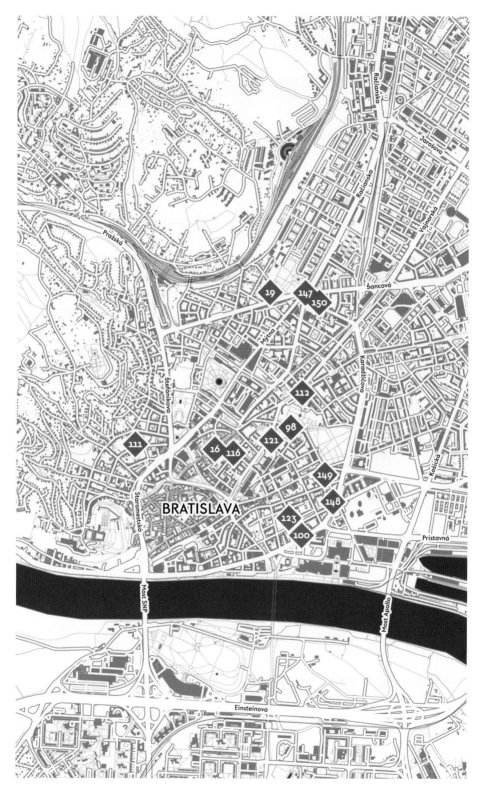

L   Bratislava | Pressburg **16, 19, 98, 100, 111, 112, 116, 121, 123, 147, 148, 149, 150**

INDEX OF BUILDINGS

GEBÄUDEREGISTER

ARCHITECTS | ARCHITEKTEN

SOURCES I QUELLEN

All of the pictures were taken between 2012 and 2017. The drawings are based on historic material taken from periodicals or monographs or found in archives. The appearance of the buildings, either as they were built or as they stand today, may differ for this reason. The original names of the buildings are listed first, with current names following in brackets. The dates give the period of construction or the date of completion and those of any significant renovations or extensions. The capital letter in brackets refers to the relevant map in this book. Dates were sourced and scrutinised with the greatest care. Uncertain entries are marked with a question mark. The architect and year of completion were not always available; the authors offer thanks in advance for any information submitted.

Sämtliche Bilder sind in den Jahren 2012 und 2017 entstanden. Grundlage der Zeichnungen ist historisches Planmaterial aus Zeitschriften, Mongrafien und Archiven. Der ausgeführte wie auch heutige Zustand weicht deshalb mitunter von den Zeichnungen ab. Bei den Gebäudebezeichnungen werden historische Namen zuerst genannt, heutige stehen in Klammern. Die Daten geben den Bauzeitraum oder das Fertigstellungsjahr der Gebäude beziehungsweise relevanter Um- oder Anbauten an. Der Großbuchstabe in Klammern verweist auf die entsprechende Karte in diesem Buch. Sämtliche Daten wurden mit höchster Sorgfalt erhoben. Unsichere Angaben sind mit einem Fragezeichen gekennzeichnet. Architekt und Baujahr waren nicht in allen Fällen zu ermitteln; die Autoren bedanken sich vorab für ergänzende Hinweise.

We would like to express special thanks for research support to | Für Unterstützung bei der Recherche danken wir: Jacek Maniecki (Bytom | Beuthen) Jakub Kowalski (Gliwice | Gleiwitz)

FURTHER READING I LITERATUR

Anonymous: Josef Gočár Hradec Králové. Vienna|Wien/Berlin 1930[?]

Anonymous: Bauten der tschechoslowakischen Kirche. Berlin 1957

Beelitz, Konstanze; Förster, Niclas: Breslau|Wrocław. Die Architektur der Moderne. Tübingen/Berlin 2006

Beil, Ralf; Dillman, Claudia (ed.|Hg.): Gesamtkunstwerk Expressionismus. Kunst, Film, Literatur, Theater, Tanz und Architektur 1905 bis 1925. Ostfildern 2010

Bolz, Hans-Stefan: Hans Poelzig und der »neuzeitliche Fabrikbau«. Industriebauten 1906–1934. Dissertation Rheinische Friedrich-Wilhelms-Universität zu Bonn 2008

Bregant, Michal et al.: Das kubistische Prag 1909–1925. Ein Stadtführer. Prague|Prag 1996

Bushart, Magdalena: Der Geist der Gotik und die expressionistische Kunst. Kunstgeschichte und Kunsttheorie 1911–1925. Munich|München 1990

Chróscicki, Julius A.; Rottermund, Andrzej: Architekturatlas von Warschau. Warsaw|Warschau 1978

Dawidowski, Robert; Długopolski, Ryszard; Szymski, Adam M.: Architektura modernistyczna lat 1928–1940 na obszarze Pomorza Zachodniego. Szczecin|Stettin 2007

Dostal, O.; Pechar, J.; Prochazka, V.: Moderní architektura v Československu. Prague|Prag 1970

Dulla, Matúš; Moravčíková, Henrieta: Architektúra Slovenska v 20. storočí. Bratislava|Pressburg 2002

Foltyn, Ladislav: Slowakische Architektur und die tschechische Avantgarde 1918–1939. Dresden 1991

Gramaccini, Norberto; Rößler, Johannes (ed.|Hg.): Hundert Jahre »Abstraktion und Einfühlung«. Konstellationen um Wilhelm Worringer. Paderborn/Munich|München 2012

Gussone, Nikolaus (ed.|Hg.): Die Architektur der Weimarer Republik in Oberschlesien. Ein Blick auf unbeachtete Bauwerke. Ratingen-Hösel 1992

Harasimonwicza, Jana (ed.|Hg.): Atlas Architektury Wrocław. 2 vols.|Bde. Wrocław|Breslau 1997/98

Havlová, Ester; Lukeš, Zdeněk: Český architektonický kubismus. Czech Architectural Cubism. Prague|Prag 2006

Herbenová, Olga; Šlapeta, Vladimir: Pavel Janák 1882–1956. Architektur und Kunstgewerbe. Prague|Prag 1984

Hnidkova, Vendula: Pavel Janák und der tschechische »Nationalstil«, in: Kritische Berichte 35 (2007), pp.|S. 75–85

Hodonyi, Robert: Herwart Waldens »Sturm« und die Architektur. Eine Analyse zur Konvergenz der Künste in der Berliner Moderne. Bielefeld 2010

Ilkosz, Jerzy: Die Jahrhunderthalle und das Ausstellungsgelände in Breslau – das Werk Max Bergs. Munich| München 2006

Ilkosz, Jerzy; Störtkuhl, Beate (ed.|Hg.): Hans Poelzig in Breslau. Architektur und Kunst 1900–1916. Delmenhorst 2000

Karasova, Daniela; Petr Krajci: Jan Kotěra 1871–1923. The Founder of Modern Czech Architecture. Prague|Prag 2001

Leśniakowska, Marta: Architekt Jan Koszczyc Witkiewicz (1881–1958) i budowanie w jego czasach. Warsaw|Warschau 1998

Leśnikowski, Wojciech (ed.|Hg.): East European Modernism. Architecture in Czechoslovakia, Hungary & Poland between the Wars. London 1996

Lukeš, Zdenek: Josef Gočár. Prague| Prag 2010.

Michalski, Sergiusz: Pawilon polski na Wystawie Sztuki Dekoracyjnej w Paryżu w 1925 roku a szklane wieże ekspresjonistów, in: De Gustibus. Studia ofiarowane przez przyjaciół Tadeuszowi Stefanowi Jaroszewskiemu z okazji 65 rocznicy urodzin, Warsaw|Warschau 1996, p.|S. 228–236

Moravánszky, Ákos: Competing Visions. Aesthetic Invention and Social Imagination in Central Europe Architecture 1867–1918. Cambridge, Massachusetts 1997

Obecní Dům Prag (ed.|Hg.): Jan Kotěra 1871–1923 The Founder of Modern Czech Architecture. Prague|Prag 2001

Odorowski, Waldemar: Architektura Katowic w latach międzywojennych 1922–1939. Katowice|Kattowitz 1994

Olszewski, Andrzej K.: Nowa forma w architekturze Polskiej 1900–1925. Teoria i praktyka. Wroclaw|Breslau/ Warsaw|Warschau/Kraków|Krakau 1967

Pehnt, Wolfgang: Die Architektur des Expressionismus. 2 Aufl. Stuttgart 1998

Pomajzlová, Alena (ed.|Hg.): Expresionismus a české umění 1905–1927. Prague|Prag 1994

Potůček, Jakub: Hradec Králové Architektura a urbanismus 1895–2009. Hradec Králové|Königgrätz 2009

Prange, Regine: Das Kristalline als Kunstsymbol. Bruno Taut und Paul Klee. Zur Reflexion des Abstrakten in Kunst und Kunsttheorie der Moderne. Hildesheim/Zurich|Zürich/New York 1991

Sellnerová, Alena; Hanzlík, Jan; Pavlíková, Marta: Architektur von Bodenbach 1900...45 Architektura Podmokel. Ústí nad Labem|Aussig 2014

Sieklicka, Aleksandra et al.: Unbekannter Modernismus. Die Architektur Oberschlesiens in der Zwischenkriegszeit. Gliwice|Gleiwitz 2012

Šlapeta, Vladimir: Jan Kotěra 1871–1921. The Founder of Modern Czech Architecture. Prague|Prag 2001

Sołtysik, Maria Jolanta; Hirsch, Robert (ed.|Hg.): Modernism in Europe – Modernism in Gdyina. Architecture of 1920s and 1930s and Its Protection. Gdyina|Gdingen 2009

Stamm, Rainer; Schreiber, Daniel (ed.|Hg.): Bau einer neuen Welt. Architektonische Visionen des Expressionismus. Cologne|Köln 2003

Stiftung Haus Schminke (ed.|Hg.): TOPOMOMO. Topographie der Bauten der Moderne. Topografie staveb moderní architektury. Cottbus 2014

Störtkuhl, Beate: Moderne Architektur in Schlesien 1900 bis 1939. Baukultur und Politik. Oldenburg 2013

Störtkuhl, Beate: Liegnitz – Die andere Moderne. Architektur der 1920er Jahre. Munich|München 2007

Švácha, Rotislav; Junek, David: Polička. Moderní architektura 1900–1950. Polička|Politschka 2007

Švácha, Rostislav: The Architecture of New Prague 1895–1945. Cambridge, Massachusetts/London 1995

Svestka, Jiri; Vlček, Tomáš: 1909–1925 Kubismus in Prag. Düsseldorf 1991

Szczerski, Andrzej: Modernizacje. Sztuka i architektura w nowych państwach Europy Środkowo-wschodniej 1918–1939. Łódź|Lodz 2010

Vesely, Dalibor: Czech New Architecture and Cubism, in: Uměni 53 (2005), p.|S. 586–604

Von Vegesack, Alexander (ed.|Hg.): Tschechischer Kubismus. Architektur und Design 1910–1925. Weil am Rhein 1991

Vybíral, Jindřich: Junge Meister. Architekten aus der Schule Otto Wagners in Mähren und Schlesien. Vienna| Wien 2007

Zubík, Martin: Slavné staby Theodora Petříka. Prague|Prag 2014

ACKNOWLEDGEMENTS I DANKSAGUNG

Once again, 'Fragments of Metropolis' has only been made possible with the help of our extraordinary friends and supporters. They drew plans, helped us with the layouts, translated texts, spread the word during the crowdfunding campaign, and finally, continually motivated us with their enthusiasm.
We thank all of you!

Auch dieses Mal ist »Fragments of Metropolis« nur durch die Unterstützung großartiger Freunde und Förderer möglich geworden. Wieder haben sie Pläne gezeichnet, uns beim Layout unterstützt, die Texte übersetzt, das Buch während des Crowdfundings bekannter gemacht, mit finanziellen Zuwendungen den Druck des Buches ermöglicht, mit ihrem Enthusiasmus uns motiviert weiterzumachen.
Danke!

SPONSORS I FÖRDERER

Robert Bosch Stiftung

SUPPORTERS I GÖNNER

Manuela Beutler &
Sabine Molls
Sebastian Claussnitzer
Markus Elmiger
Bruno Fritschi
Lukas Hoffleit
Friederike Jenderek
Alexander Jungi
Eva-Maria &
Jens N. Daldrop
Lilian & Lutz Kögler
Frank Köhler
Irène Kramer
Petra & Olaf Lehmann

nightnurse images
Thomas Nölleke
Marc-Olivier Paux
Michael Rabe
Frauke Ries
Mathias Rinka
Jutta Romberg
Daniel Romer
Carolin Sämisch
Fjona Scherkamp
Benjamin Sieber
Annabel & Franz
von Wietersheim
Clemens Zirkelbach

IMPRINT | IMPRESSUM

Hirmer Verlag GmbH
Nymphenburger Straße 84
80636 Munich | München

CONCEPT | KONZEPT
Niels Lehmann, Christoph Rauhut

LAYOUT | GESTALTUNG
Niels Lehmann, Christoph Rauhut

TRANSLATION | ÜBERSETZUNG
Philip Shelley

COPY-EDITING | LEKTORAT
Tanja Bokelmann

PROOFREADING | KORREKTORAT
Michael Pilewski (English), Tanja Bokelmann (Deutsch)

PRINTING, BINDING, LITHOGRAPHY | DRUCK, BINDUNG, LITHOGRAFIE
Westermann Druck Zwickau GmbH

PAPER | PAPIER
Profi matt 150g/m²

TYPEFACES | SCHRIFTEN
Koban 3000, BA13

PICTURES | ABBILDUNGEN
Text Störtkuhl: Abb. 1: Archive|Archiv Nordost-Institut, Lüneburg; Abb. 2: Anna Prokopová;
Abb. 3: Deutsche Bauzeitung 58 (1924), p.|S. 623; Abb. 4: Archive|Archiv Beate Störtkuhl;
Abb. 5: Czesław Pietraszko, Legnica/Lignitz; Abb. 6: Archive|Archiv Beate Störtkuhl
Study for a facade | Fassadenstudie: © Private collection, Berlin
All other pictures | Alle weiteren Abbildungen: © Niels Lehmann

DRAWINGS | ZEICHNUNGEN
Dennis Arendt, Annina Baumgartner, Kristina Bindernagel, Daria Blaschkiewitz, Jens Daldrop, Jenny
Dittrich, Nicole Gamisch, Felix Greiner-Petter, Michael Grunitz, Andres Herzog, Niels Lehmann,
Stephan Liebscher, Ties Linders, Hannes Mahlknecht, Evgenia Pronina, Michael Rabe, Christoph
Rauhut, Jutta Romberg, Hannes Rutenfranz, Petra Schwyter, Nils Tennhoff, Florian Summa, Clemens
Wagner, Christine Wilkening-Aumann, Karl Wruck

MAPS | KARTEN
© OpenStreetMap contributors, CC-BY-SA

ISBN 978-3-7774-3092-8

www.hirmerverlag.de | www.hirmerpublishers.com
www.fragmentsofmetropolis.eu

Biliographic Information published by the Deutsche Nationalbibliothek
The Deutsche Nationalbibliothek lists this publication in the Deutsche Nationalbibliografie; detailed
bibliographic data is available on the internet at http://dnb.d-nb.de.

Biliografische Information der Deutschen Nationalbibliothek
Die Deutsche Nationalbibliothek verzeichnet diese Publikation in der Deutschen Nationalbibliografie;
detaillierte bibliografische Daten sind im Internet über http://dnb.d-nb.de abrufbar.